D1005974

Protecting Your Children Online

Protecting Your Children Online

What You Need to Know about Online Threats to Your Children

Kimberly Ann McCabe

ROWMAN & LITTLEFIELD
Lanham • Boulder • New York • London

Published by Rowman & Littlefield
A wholly owned subsidiary of The Rowman & Littlefield Publishing Group, Inc.
4501 Forbes Boulevard, Suite 200, Lanham, Maryland 20706
www.rowman.com

Unit A, Whitacre Mews, 26-34 Stannary Street, London SE11 4AB

British Library Cataloguing in Publication Information Available

Library of Congress Cataloging-in-Publication Data
978-1-4422-7466-2 (cloth)
978-1-4422-7467-9 (ebook)

♾™ The paper used in this publication meets the minimum requirements
of American National Standard for Information Sciences—Permanence
of Paper for Printed Library Materials, ANSI/NISO Z39.48-1992.

Printed in the United States of America

For my parents, Jim and Shirley McCabe

Contents

Foreword

Captain Michael Harmony

Kimberly McCabe's *Protecting Your Children in Cyberspace: What Parents Need to Know* is a must-have book for parents wishing to protect their children from Internet Crimes Against Children. As a law enforcement officer with nearly two decades of experience in investigating Internet child exploitation cases and as an individual who has served as the chairperson for the US Department of Justice's Internet Crimes Against Children National Task Force, it has become apparent that we are witnessing the unique union of a powerful technology age and an awakening of child vulnerabilities by individuals wishing to abuse children within this virtual world. *Protecting Your Children in Cyberspace: What Parents Need to Know* is an instant success as it not only identifies specific crimes involving children within the online community but also provides parents the information they need to ensure the safety of their children even in cases where their children places themselves in a potentially harmful setting.

Within this book, crimes such as child corruption, child pornography, cyberbullying, cyberstalking, and sextortion are discussed in detail, include definitions of these crimes, and most importantly, the legislation enacted within the United States to address such crimes. In addition, historical and specific cases of child victimization are detailed to provide parents information for discussions on the topics with their children.

While US presidential histories suggest that the Age of Reagan focused upon the War on Drugs, the Age of Bush Jr. focused on terrorism, and the Age of Obama racial inequalities, child victimization via cyberspace has yet to be recognized. Kimberly McCabe's work focuses on the vulnerabilities of all children regardless of the gender, race, and economic standing. Her discussions on the various crimes and the dynamics that exist prior to the victimization of children bring to the forefront the power of parenting in establishing lines of communication and limitation in the actions of their children. Hence, central to the themes of this book is the responsibility of parents in establishing and enforcing boundaries for the children and the acknowledgment that many of these crimes involving children in cyberspace may be preventable through the proactive actions of parents. This book is a must-read for parents wishing to protect their children and for parents with questions regarding cyberspace and the dangers to their children.

Preface

As a parent of two children and a professor of criminology, my children have grown up with the consistent message of "stay safe" and the repeated question of "What would you do if . . . ?" Many years ago, the significance of my many parent and child conversations was apparent when my son, who was probably about five years old at the time and attending one of my crime prevention lectures, stunned my class of undergraduate students as he answered one of my "What would you do?" questions before any of those enrolled in the class could respond. From an educator's perspective, I was pleased. From a mom's perspective, I was ecstatic. I had provided my son the information he may someday need to stay safe and he remembered those words.

This book is not for everyone. When my daughter was young, she would often ask why I always wrote about the bad things people did to children. My explanation was always that I did not want any more children hurt and that most people do not want to talk, much less write, about child abuse. This book is for those parents and grandparents who are concerned about cyberspace and the potential dangers that this new environment facilitates for our children. For many years, I have written books for young, college-aged students. This book is written for parents like me who have questions about the risks to their children within the online community and the reality of those Internet Crimes Against Children. It is my desire that this book will provide you the information needed to begin and continue talking with your children over the course of their childhood to better protect them from individuals within cyberspace who wish to exploit and abuse them. After all, a parent's responsibility is the safety and protection of their children. I hope this book helps.

Acknowledgments

No one person writes a book. There are individuals and experiences throughout the author's life that motivate and inspire and there are individuals who challenge and confront. These colleagues, family, friends, and publisher supported this effort in ways that far exceeded my expectation and I want to acknowledge those individuals—the ones who convinced me of the importance of this book. So I would first like to acknowledge my wonderful parents, James and Shirley McCabe, who not only provided me with what some would consider a "picture-perfect" childhood, but also provided me the courage to succeed and fail in life; and my children, Jessica and Mac, who remind me daily of the reality of childhood and the teen years.

As I mentioned in the preface, the five books I have written before this book were intended to be used as textbooks within a college course. When approached by a representative of Rowman and Littlefield Publishers, Kathryn Knigge, for a book on child abuse, I, frankly, was ready to try something new. When I sent her my initial proposal, her words were "it reads like a textbook." Her words caused panic in me. I did not know if I could write a book for individuals outside of the area of criminology. Ms. Knigge helped me outline this parents' book and the topics seemed natural; however, I was a bit anxious about the writing. My colleagues, Dr. Julius Sigler, Dr. Annette Evans, and Dr. Elza Tiner, who were not professors of criminology (but professors of physics, religious studies, and Latin, respectively), encouraged me to try this new focus. As one of my colleagues suggested, "Kim, just write the book like you're talking to me"—that is how I have attempted to write this book, from one parent to another, for the common goal of our children.

There are so many other individuals who have provided me the encouragement and stories for a book such as this one. Those individuals include Captain Mike Harmony and Sheriff Mike Brown of the Southern Virginia Internet Crimes Against Children Task Force (Bedford County Sheriff's Office, Virginia), and Dan Murphy, another retired cop and colleague who specialized in the investigations of crimes against children and many others. Thank you.

Chapter One

Introducing Cyberspace and Internet Crimes against Children

Sandy's daughter is a cheerleader. One evening, while attending the local high school football game, Sandy notices two others parents involved in a conversation, glancing at her while they discuss their subject of interest. Both parents are friends of Sandy's; however, neither is acknowledging her presence at the game. During halftime, one of the parents approached Sandy for a private conversation. During their conversation, the parent reveals to Sandy that a seminude picture of her daughter is being circulated around the high school and she saw it on her son's cell phone.

As a parent, our main concern is the safety and protection of our children. We teach our children to look both ways before they cross the street. We teach our children to be cautious around fire and sharp objects. And we teach our children about "stranger danger." All of this is to ensure a happy, safe, and fulfilled childhood. Unfortunately, in today's world of instant information and Internet searches, we often fail to teach our children about the dangers of cyberspace. For clarity, cyberspace is the domain in which individuals utilize computers and other electronic devices to communicate via Internet or cell phone providers. The term, which became popular in the 1990s, is now used to describe anything associated with the online community.

This book is designed to be used as an information source for parents attempting to protect their children from victimization in cyberspace. Specifically, the purpose of this book is to provide parents information on the characteristics of cyberspace and the online community as well as Internet Crimes Against Children (ICAC). In addition, this book will provide protective strategies for parents to reduce the likelihood of their child's victimization and definitions for a variety of ICAC, which will be discussed as related to their various risk factors for children and profiles of perpetrators. Finally, also included in this book is information on laws designed to protect children within cyberspace and tips for parents wishing to discuss the topics of sexual exploitation and victimization with their children as associated with ICAC.

In September 2016, a fourteen-year-old New York male was arrested for setting a woman's clothes on fire.[1] The woman was wearing traditional Muslim garb. In January 2016, a thirteen-year-old Virginia female was killed after meeting her eighteen-year-old "boyfriend" who she had met online.[2] In 2015, a thirty-one-year-old former veteran of Iraq was convicted of posing as a teenager on the Internet, and extorting young girls into sending him sexually graphic photos of themselves and each other.[3] In 2010, an eighteen-year-old male from New Jersey jumped to his death after being a victim of cyberbullying.[4] Every year, more and more children and teens are victims of ICAC. This is certainly a concern for parents. Each year, more and more children and teens are enticed through technology into actions they would not normally perform. Each year, more and more children and teens are the victims of sexual exploitation or child pornography via the Internet. Each year, the role of technology increases in the lives of our children. For some children those increases are not always positive.

There are those who suggest that the term pornography should be used for materials that depict adults engaged in consensual sexual acts;[5] hence, the phrase "child pornography" does not reflect the seriousness of this abuse of children. Therefore, much of the research on ICAC represented in this book will refer to those abuses as child sexual exploitation or child sexual activity; however, when utilized, the phrase child pornography is abhorrent and significant.

For parents, one of their worst nightmares is that someone will cause harm to their children. For many, the statement of "say what you want about me but don't say a word about my child" rings true. From the moment our children are born until the moment we die, we want to protect our children, help our children, and love our children. With that in mind, as a parent, we must be ready to educate our children on the potential use of technology in their victimization. All cases previously mentioned involved crimes against or involving children. All cases involved either the Internet or a cell phone. All cases involved someone's child or children.

Since the first written recording of history, children have been abused or neglected by their parents, grandparents, siblings, acquaintances, and strangers. As documented in the Hebrew Bible or Old Testament, Abraham considers the sacrifice of his son Isaac,[6] Lot impregnates both of his daughters,[7] and Tamar is raped by her half-brother.[8] However, it was not until the late 1800s that the abuse of children became a focus in US courts.[9]

Media accounts suggest that US efforts to address child abuse began in the 1870s with a case of child abuse and neglect in New York. In 1875, the rights of legal intervention were extended for the protection of children with the Prevention of Cruelty to Children Act.[10] However, it was not until the publicity of the 1996 Christmas murder of six-year-old Jon Benet Ramsey in Boulder, Colorado, that the public and media began to focus their attention on the abuse and victimization of children.[11]

Currently, with approximately three million children identified as victims of child abuse on an annual basis in the United States, American efforts have focused on child abuse in terms of awareness, education, and legal efforts. Today, child exploitation through the Internet or cyberspace is receiving not only the attention of abusers, but also the attention of parents, legal practitioners, and the public.

For clarity, the term child abuse refers to victimizations that are divided into four specific categories.[12] Those categories are: (1) physical abuse, (2) sexual abuse, (3) emotional abuse, and (4) neglect. Physical abuse refers to actions that result in injuries to the child. Sexual abuse includes, but is not limited to, intercourse with a child, child exploitation, and child pornography. Emotional abuse refers to a pattern of psychologically destructive behaviors that result in the reduction of the child's self-esteem. Included in these categories of abuse are the actions of terrorizing, isolation of, and the corruption of the child. Finally, neglect refers to an adult's inability to provide for the child's basic needs of survival to include food, shelter, medical treatment, and safety.

The majority of the crimes against children in cyberspace are usually classified under the categories of either child sexual abuse or emotional abuse. Research conducted by the Centers for Disease Control suggests that approximately one in three girls and one in six boys are sexually abused before they reach the age of eighteen. In addition, approximately 40 percent of those child victims will not exhibit any physical symptoms;[13] however, they will still suffer serious long-term consequences resulting from that abuse. Sexual abuse in cyberspace reflects similar statistics; however, emotional abuse, which results from crimes such as cyberbullying, and sextortion are more likely to be reported and documented with ICAC than traditional off-line cases of emotional abuse.[14]

As a parent, we presume that our child, if harmed, will reveal to us their victimization; however, that presumption is often not correct in that child victims rarely provide clear accounts of their abuse and many children only subtly imply that something may have happened to them. If we, as a parent, miss even one hint of disclosed victimization, our child may not receive the help they need. Hence, it is critical for parents to be aware of the risks associated with child victimization as well as the potentially faint disclosures to better protect our children.

Adam Walsh,[15] Jacob Wetterling,[16] Polly Klaas,[17] and Megan Kanka[18] are all well-known historical cases of child sexual abuse. However, those cases are considered "old school" as none of those cases involved cyberspace and the Internet. Hence, cyberspace is a new location for predators seeking to abuse children.

It is not unusual to read reports or view television shows focused on children being victimized by predators on the Internet or what is commonly referred to as ICAC. The Internet, thought to be one of our most life-changing inventions designed to provide individuals instant access to information, now provides individuals instant access to other individuals; many of those other individuals are children. Hence, today the Internet, which allows predators the opportunity to target young people who they have not met in person, plays a significant role in the sexual and emotional abuse of our children.

For those who study the victimization of children and for those who work with child victims, it is expected that the majority of the cases of child abuse are from perpetrators within the family. This is rarely the case for crimes against children or teens that involve the Internet or the online community. Therefore, as a guide for parents attempting to protect their children from victimization within the online community, this book emphasizes the roles of technology as related to child abuse and exploitation. Specifically, this book is dedicated to providing parents information on ICAC as the other dangers of cyberspace as related to the protection of their children.

ICAC include but are not limited to child pornography, child solicitation, cyberbullying, cyberstalking, and sexting. In addition, the Internet and technology are used in other aspects of child exploitation to include enticing children, corrupting children, and long-term victimization crimes such as child sex rings and child trafficking. For clarity, child pornography is defined as a photo, film, or other visual representation of a person under the age of eighteen engaged in sexual activity or a photo, film, or other visual representation of the genitalia of a person under the age of eighteen.[19] Cyberbullying is defined as the repeated harassment of threatening or embarrassing pictures through the use of a computer, cell phone, or other electronic devices.[20] Cyberstalking is defined as the repeated use of electronic community to harass, stalk, or frighten someone.[21] Sexting is defined as the sending or receiving of sexually suggestive images or messages through a cell phone.[22] Enticement is defined as the persuasion or extortion of a child into actions they would not normally perform.[23] Corruption is defined as the encouragement of destructive or antisocial behaviors.[24] A child sex ring usually involves multiple child victims and multiple adult perpetrators.[25] Child trafficking is generally defined as the harboring or movement of children against their will and their guardian's will to participate in criminal activities.[26] Unfortunately, each of these actions is common in today's virtual world. Each of these actions involves children, and each of these child-involved actions is illegal.

HISTORICAL EFFORTS TO REDUCE CHILD ABUSE

Nearly a century after the Prevention of Cruelty to Children Act, federal and state governments in the United States began to address the issue of child abuse. In 1972, the National Center for the Prevention of Child Abuse and Neglect[27] was established to provide education on the issue of child abuse and to train public servants in its recognition and prevention.

In 1974, the Child Abuse Prevention and Treatment Act (CAPT) specifically defined the actions of child abuse. In 1978, the CAPT was revised to include language related to abandoned infants and became known as the Child Abuse Prevention and Treatment and Adoption Reform Act. In 1985, the Child Protection Act identified the topic of child pornography and the penalties for those engaged in this form of child sexual exploitation. In 1992, the Child Abuse, Domestic Violence, Adoption and Family Service Act provided for services to victims of family abuse. In 1994, the Violent Crime Control and Law Enforcement Act established a sex offender registry. In 1996, the Telecommunications Reform Act and the Child Pornography Protection Act attempted to regulate information dispersed over the Internet and included penalties for child pornography. In 2006, the Adam Walsh Child Protection and Reform Act led to sex offender registries and[28] in 2014 the Preventing Sex Trafficking and Strengthening Families Act acknowledged the presence of the online community and the need for victims' services in the severe victimization of children. However, few if any researchers or practitioners could have predicted the negative consequences to children as a result of the introduction of the Internet to our daily lives in cyberspace.

HISTORY OF INTERNET
CRIMES AGAINST CHILDREN

In 1993, a federal investigation in Maryland identified two suspects who had sexually exploited at least twenty-five children. Within the investigation, it was revealed that cyberspace was utilized to transmit sexually explicit images to lure minors into engaging in illicit sexual activity. In 1995, as a result of that investigation, Innocent Images National Initiative, a part of the Cyber Division, was created within the FBI. In 2000, the Crimes Against Children Program was created to provide assistance to local and state law enforcement agencies. In 2012, the Crimes Against Children Program and the Innocent Images National Initiative merged to form the Division of Violent Crimes Against Children, with the goals of the protection of children and services for victims.

Hence, the actions to reduce ICAC, originally started in 1998 as a task force by the Office of Juvenile Justice and Delinquency Prevention (OJJDP) to provide state and local law enforcement agencies, the tools to combat Internet crime against children.[29] Today, this task force initiative has resulted in multiagency cooperation, education, and training to law enforcement and others who work with victims to combat ICAC. At one time, the ICAC Task Force focused exclusively on the distribution of child pornography and those perpetrators. Today, the ICAC Task Force now includes such crimes as cyberbullying, child enticement, and sextortion in addition to child pornography.

Today, many law enforcement agencies operate specialized units that focus on ICAC. In addition, prosecutors are educated on laws and practices related to ICAC. Investigations are initiated through citizen complaints, reports by Internet Service Providers (ISP), cyber tips to the National Center for Missing and Exploited Children (NCMEC), law enforcement referrals, and by uncovering names of online location chatrooms that suggest illegal activity. However, in the majority of the cases of ICAC, the victimization of the child or teen could have be prevented or detected earlier if parents were able to identify risk factors or the crimes against their children.

TYPES OF INTERNET
CRIMES AGAINST CHILDREN

The majority of the perpetrators of traditional cases of child abuse are family members or *familia*. This is not the case for ICAC as in the majority of these cases the perpetrators are what is called *extrafamilial* or someone outside of the family.[30] Ironically, extrafamilial abuse is the category of child abuse that was historically the most likely to be reported to the police; however, the use of cyberspace creates a difficult environment for the detection of such crimes and often results in nondetection and, therefore, the nonreporting of ICAC. Hence, in most cases of ICAC, it is the parent of the child or teen that is in the best position to detect the victimization of their child. As the role of the parent is critical in preventing ICAC, parents must be familiar with technology and the risks to their children as associated with ICAC. The following are a general summary of the ICAC discussed in this book for parents.

Child Corruption

Individuals use the Internet and the online community to corrupt and recruit children for a variety of actions, including the perpetuation of hate. In these instances groups affiliated with a variety of organizations attempt to persuade children and teens to continue their actions of discrimination, actions, or acts of bias and hate against targeted groups of individuals. Included within the most common groups or movements used to facilitate hate are Anarchists,[31] #BlackLivesMatter,[32] KKK,[33] Nation of Islam,[34] and the New Black Panthers.[35] Each of the groups (or movements) operates under the First Amendment rights to free speech, freedom of the press, and freedom to assemble; however, they entice teens to participate in violent protests or actions that victimize groups of individuals based upon some demographic characteristics such as race, religion, sexual orientation, or political attitude.

As parents, we must acknowledge the vulnerabilities of our children. Included within these vulnerabilities is the ease with which many young people may be persuaded by the influences of their peers and the online media. Therefore, open lines of communication are necessary in reducing the risk for child corruption by the online community. Hence, with an increase in criminal incidents of hate by young individuals, a concern for many parents should be child corruption.

Child Pornography

Research suggests that today's child pornography is often the result of peer-to-peer contact or networks.[36] Offenders involved in these activities are typically younger than most offenders of traditional accounts of child sexual abuse. Hence, the stereotypical white, suspicious-looking male in the forty-to-fifty age range probably does not apply. However, research suggests that the pedophiles (individuals who act upon their sexual attractions to the physical characteristics of children) aggressively target specific victim types; today, most of those targeted victims utilize the Internet. Those victims are our children.

During February 1996, President Bill Clinton signed the Telecommunications Reform Act, which included regulatory reform and obscenity prohibitions.[37] Imbedded within the Telecommunications Reform Act is the Communications Decency Act (CDA)—an attempt to censor the Internet of obscene, indecent, or annoying communications written or otherwise, and imposes penalties on those convicted of CDA violations.[38] Unfortunately, as is the case with ICAC, the enforceability of the Telecommunications Reform Act is difficult if not nearly impossible as the Internet is a global community without boundaries,[39] with technology that changes daily, with millions of online users every day, and with no clear police jurisdictions of authority existing. Hence, we have a law with little practical ability for enforcement.

In cases of pornography as in ICAC, offenders may use the online community to victimize directly through the production of child pornography or indirectly in the distribution of child pornography for economic gain. For those offenders most interested in child pornography for economic gain, parents must acknowledge that their child is perceived (by their abusers) as simply a product for consumption and not a vulnerable human being with individual rights and protections.

Unfortunately, for those victims of child pornography, the never-ending cycle of Internet posts, access, and distribution equates to the revictimization of the child or teen. Hence, in many cases children and teen victims feel as though this abuse will never end. Parents, unable to end the abuse, feel frustrated and hopeless in this aspect of child protection. Therefore, cyberspace is an area of concern for parents interested in protecting their children from online victimization.

Child Sex Rings

In general, the ICAC of sex rings involves multiple children and multiple adult abusers.[40] However, there exist solo sex rings which involve multiple child victims and one (usually young adult male) offender. Through this type of ICAC, there is sexual activity among all involved as abusers often utilize the Internet to identify child victims based upon desired physical characteristics such as age and gender. The access of children for a sex ring is not a crime of opportunity but a crime which results from planning. Again, much of this identification of victims is within cyberspace. Included in the items of trade for sex rings is not only sexual activity but also child pornography. These child victims are forced to participate in sexual activities with either the adult perpetrators or other children within the sex ring. Hence, sex rings should also be of concern for parents.

Child Sex Tourism

Sex tourism involves the traveling of adults to locations outside of their home country for the intent to engage in any form of sexual contact with minors. Child sex tourism results in the physical, sexual, and emotional abuse of victims.[41] Although advertised as fishing or hunting tours in cyberspace, sex tourism provides large financial gains for those involved in the recruiting and managing of children. Hence, communications among offenders occur over the Internet where abusers plan their involvement in the child sex ring or organize or assist other persons in traveling for this purpose. Therefore, child sex tours should be of concern for parents.

Child Solicitation

One of the greatest advantages in today's world of technology is the access to individuals throughout the world. Unfortunately, this is also one of the worst aspects of technology as related to ICAC. The computer or cell phone provides individuals the opportunities to interact with each other. Unfortunately, for these individuals wishing to contact a child the opportunity for an interaction also exists. Pedophiles engage children for many purposes to include the opportunity for a sexual chat. These perpetrators, skilled at initiating conversations with teens or children, can use an array of strategies to engage in sexual conduct with a minor. Parents should recognize that these initial exchanges are not always sexual in nature and include talking about animals, the environment, or even the unfairness of parents. Thus, the Internet is an invaluable tool for individuals who wish to engage young people and prey on young victims. In addition, sexual predators are able to access chat lines to communicate with other adults who share their same fantasies of child exploitation.

It is suggested that there are approximately forty thousand websites dedicated to the support of adult–child sexual relations.[42] It is through these websites that predators engage other abusers in conversations on how to best talk to (or solicit) a child or teenager into participating in an activity such as a sexual encounter. Hence, parents must be aware of the methods by which a perpetrator may solicit their child.

Through the anonymity of websites and chatrooms, predators can pretend to be the same age as the child and hence bond with the child as they provide false information about themselves or the interests they may share. Using this tactic they are able to, at times, convince the child or teen to physically meet with them in a location of convenience. Other adult offenders may not falsify their age and may admit to their age while befriending the child through flattery and expressing mutual interest in whatever will enhance their bond. Finally, some offenders may openly solicit a child to engage in sexual conduct (sometimes for money) and formulate plans to meet with them despite the fact that the child, through their Internet chat, has revealed that he or she is under the legal age to consent to having sex. In direct cases of child solicitation such as these, law enforcement officers, working in an undercover capacity, have posed as children or other child sex offenders to lure unsuspecting predators into custody. It is also these direct cases of child solicitation that are most often reported to police by parents. Hence, parents must be able to recognize child solicitation in cyberspace.

Child Trafficking

Humans are trafficked for a variety of reasons—the two most common are sex and labor.[43] Research suggests that approximately one million people are trafficked annually across the globe with approximately 50 percent of those victims under the age of eighteen. Hence, the trafficking of children refers to the category of trafficking identified in the 2003 Trafficking Victims Protection Reauthorization Act (TVPRA) as a severe form of trafficking.[44]

Included under the reasons for child trafficking are, as with adult cases, for sex and labor, but children are also trafficked for other reasons to include adoptions, drug smuggling, and for healthy organs. For the most part, child trafficking is an economically based ICAC. The motivation is money and many of the contacts and victims required for trafficking are located within cyberspace.

Although parents in the United States often equate child trafficking with underdeveloped countries, we must acknowledge that child trafficking does occur in the United States and that many of the victims of child trafficking are US citizens. As parents, it is essential that we are aware of not only the actions and locations of our children, but also the actions of other children within our communities. Hence, as a parent, it is essential to be aware of the illegal activity of child trafficking and the role of cyberspace in child victimization.

Cyberbullying

When asked about violence within the school environment, one of the biggest concerns for parents is bullying and cyberbullying.[45] Cyberbullying is essentially the bullying of an individual through computers and other electronic devices. Cyberbullying relies on technological programs such as email, websites, and chat rooms to intimidate, to embarrass, or to humiliate their victim. Other types of cyberbullying can include posting embarrassing or compromising pictures where a child's face may be attached to a pornographic picture. Once these pictures are posted, they can no longer be retrieved, therefore leaving the victim with a constant reminder of their victimization. As a parent of a child being cyberbullied, your first instinct is often to involve a school official. However, although the first incident of bullying may have been initiated in the school environment, the action of cyberbullying has extended its reach far beyond the classroom.

Incidents of cyberbullying, just as with incidents of bullying, are more likely to occur in middle school.[46] Although both males and females are perpetrators of cyberbullying, some suspect that in cases of male and female interactions, males are the perpetrators of cyberbullying and females the victims. However, additional studies have shown that females are twice as likely as males to be both the perpetrator and the recipient of cyberbullying actions.[47]

Victims of cyberbullying are similar to the victims of bullying in that they are often social isolates, disliked by their peers, children with disabilities, or members of the lesbian, gay, bisexual, or transsexual (LGBT) community. In addition, if a child is a victim of bullying, they are also likely to be a victim of cyberbullying. Parents, when asked, are often very concerned about their child being bullied in cyberspace.

Cyberstalking

The repeated use of technology to monitor, harass, intimidate, coerce, or frighten someone into an unwilling action is what many refer to as cyberstalking.[48] Unlike stalking (or physical stalking), which has resulted in a variety of laws for prevention, cyberstalking relies upon the anonymity of the Internet and the online community to protect the perpetrator. Thus, the apprehension of a cyberstalker is much more difficult than a physical stalker.

Parents should be aware that although most see stalking and cyberstalking as adult crimes, young people and especially teens in "dating relationships" may be cyberstalked through tracking devices and other forms of technology.[49] Examples of cyberstalking also include posting inappropriate or offensive comments under the name of the victim, sending threatening emails to a victim or the victim's family, and subscribing the victim to pornography or other unwanted electronic sites. Hence, cyberstalking is a concern for parents with children socializing in cyberspace.

Gross Sexual Imposition

Sexual imposition or gross sexual imposition is another type of ICAC. This crime results when a perpetrator forces two individuals to have sexual contact with each other against their will.[50] In these cases, the forced sexual activity is not with the perpetrator; however, the perpetrator often observes and records the activity to later watch again or to distribute via the Internet. The phrase gross sexual imposition is reserved for those cases with victims under the age of thirteen. Sexual imposition is more of a general phrase for the illegal activity. Hence, this form of ICAC carries not only the immediate consequence of sexual abuse but also the long-term consequence of emotional abuse through sexual exploitation and parents must be aware of this form of abuse in cyberspace.

Sexting

Statistics indicate that over 80 percent of all US teens have their own cell phones and many send text messages. Those text messages are sometimes considered sext messages.[51] Sexting is vaguely defined to include the sending or receiving of sexual images; however, state laws generally focus only on the nude or seminude pictures of minors and only if the images are reported to law enforcement by parents. Thus, it is the parent's duty to educate and protect their child or teen from the vulnerabilities which exist from sexting. Unlike adults, teens without the capacity to make rational choice decisions are often the main perpetrators of sexting. Those teens who generally send the original sext messages are females.

Those teens who distribute the sext message for the first time are usually males. Unfortunately and rarely considered at the time of the original sext, there are multiple risks to the victim from sexting after the original message is sent.

In general, teens who have participated in sexting place themselves at risk for other forms of victimization. Specifically, many teens who have sexted a message to one certain individual may later discover that their "private" picture message has now been viewed by hundreds of individuals within the online community; thus, a teenager who thought a nude picture of themselves or a sexually provocative message would be an appropriate "gift" for their romantic partner is now a victim of child pornography. In addition, teens who have sexted messages may also find themselves victims of harassment, cyberstalking, or sextortion by an individual or individuals who have viewed their message. Also, teens who have sexted may find themselves "outed" in a community which may not respect or support their lifestyle or choices. Finally, teens that have sexted another may find themselves victims of identity theft or impersonation on sites such as Facebook with the blame or responsibilities for another's actions placed on them. From a prevention perspective, it is critical for parents to acknowledge that sexuality is a part of becoming an adult and to explain to their children or teens the dangers associated with sexting. In addition, parents should be concerned about their child's activities if sexting in cyberspace.

Sextortion

The crime of sextortion involves the use of the computer to obtain through coercion sexual dialogues or pornography from another. In many cases, the victims are teens. Unlike consensual sexual activities, with cases of sextortion, an offender, who essentially enters the home of a child or teen electronically or through interactions via cell phones, demands the production of sexual materials such as videos or images by the victim.

According to the US Justice Department, sextortion is one of the most significantly growing threats against children within the online community.[52] As a parent, one must be aware that there are individuals within the online community who will threaten or coerce a child or teen into performing sexual acts to be shared with everyone in the virtual world. Hence, sextortion is essentially blackmail in cyberspace and should be of concern to parents.

A PARENT'S ROLE

For any parent, their role is to provide for the safety of their child. Included within that role is the acknowledgment of risk factors for the child as a potential victim of ICAC. Those risk factors, discussed later in this book, include children or teens with low self-esteem and poor impulse control. In addition, children or teens who witness violence in the home or substance abuse within the home are also risk factors for teen victims of ICAC. Finally, stressful life events such as marital problems and parental or sibling illnesses are also risk factors for child victims of ICAC.

With crimes against children that involve the Internet, the parental role is consistent—protect their child. Unfortunately, with ICAC, the visibility most often present with perpetrators of child abuse is not apparent. This lack of a clear problem provides even more of a difficult task for the parent. Children, and especially teens, are attempting to assert their independence from their parents. Unfortunately, their assertions occur within an online community with individuals waiting to target these young individuals. A parent's role, just like the technology, must continually change and adjust to the changes of technological advances. This book attempts to provide parents the tools they need to begin to protect their children from individuals utilizing the online community to target children and teens.

Again, as a parent, our main concern is the safety and protection of our children. We teach them to look both ways as they cross the street and we teach them about "stranger danger." Unfortunately, in today's world of instant information and searches through the Internet, we fail to teach our children about ICAC to include child pornography, child solicitation, cyberbullying, cyberstalking, sextortion, sexting, child corruption, and child trafficking. This book is the beginning of a process of awareness and education for parents attempting to protect their children from ICAC.

SUMMARY

Cyberspace has created a new environment for the victimization of children. Unfortunately, for many parents, their concern is not without merit. As more and more children enter cyberspace, more and more children are participating in online conversations and sexting with individuals interested in not only their friendship but also exploitation.

Parents must be aware of the ICAC that exist within cyberspace. In particular, parents must be aware of the crimes in cyberspace such as child pornography, cyberbullying, and sextortion as well as the risk that these crimes pose to their children. As parents, our main concern is the safety and protection of our children. Unfortunately, we often fail to teach our children about the dangers of cyberspace. This book is designed to be used as a reference for parents attempting to protect their children from victimization in cyberspace.

Chapter Two

Welcome to Children and Cyberspace

During dinner, Leanne notices that her daughter Jordan is unusually quiet, eats very little of her dinner, and has been in her room all evening with her door closed. After cleaning the kitchen, she enters her daughter's room to check on her. Immediate Jordan begins crying and shows Leanne her Facebook page. Posted on Jordan's page are pictures of her daughter kissing a female classmate. According to Jordan, the image was not posted by her.

Technology has improved so many aspects of modern living. Medical advances have increased lifespans and lowered infant mortality rates. Travel occurs within hours not weeks. Information is available at the touch of a button. Unfortunately, technology has also promoted the vulnerabilities for victims in a variety of modalities. This includes an increase in the vulnerability of children in cyberspace. Welcome to cyberspace—for many, the best and worst invention to date. Cyberspace is amazing. It allows children to learn, to connect with others, and to explore ideas and facts. Unfortunately, cyberspace also provides for another environment in which individuals interested in child exploitation may identify, select, and abuse their victims. This chapter will highlight what parents should know as they enter the world of children and technology. In particular, this chapter is a discussion on what parents might expect as their children enter into relationships via cyberspace, information on the perpetrators of ICAC, a general overview of terminology utilized within cyberspace, and the parents' role in the introduction of their child to the online world to help that child avoid victimization.

For many parents and grandparents, cyberspace is a mystery. Their knowledge of technology comes from their children. Therefore, if parents desire to protect their children from victimization in cyberspace, they must know the advantages, disadvantages, rewards, and risks to their children for the use of the online community.

In 2016, a thirteen-year-old Virginia girl left her home to meet the eighteen-year-old online boyfriend.[1] Her body was found three days later. In 2015, a thirty-one-year-old former Top Gun Navy instructor and veteran of the Iraqi War, was convicted of posing as a teenager on the Internet, and extorted young girls into sending him sexually graphic photos of themselves engaged in sexual activities.[2] Also in 2015, three Michigan high school teens were found guilty of sexting multiple nude and semi-nude images of their peers;[3] hence, sexting images of child pornography. In 2011, a twelve-year-old was convicted and sentenced for cyberstalking after posting sexually explicit messages on her classmate's Facebook page.[4] In 2006, a thirteen-year-old Missouri teen, who was a victim of cyberbullying, hanged herself in a bedroom closet.[5] Each of these cases involved crimes against children. Each of these cases resulted in negative long-term consequences. And each of these cases involved the Internet, a cell phone, or both. Hence, each of these cases involved children and cyberspace. Today, the Internet, originally designed to benefit society, now provides individuals access to and communications among other individuals, which includes predators focused on the abuse and exploitation of children.

Over the years, children such as Adam Walsh,[6] Jacob Wetterling,[7] Polly Klaas,[8] and Megan Kanka[9] have all been victims of sexual abuse and all with the most tragic of consequences that have led to legislative efforts and increased public awareness in the area of child victimization and, in particular, child sexual abuse. However, none of these historical cases involved cyberspace or lines of communications with their predators prior to their victimization. Therefore, ICAC, that often begin with interactions between perpetrators and their child victims, are now the most common worries for parents as related to the safety of their children.

WHAT CAN I AS A PARENT EXPECT?

Just as there exists specific terminology for perpetrators of child abuse, there exists specific terminology for predators within cyberspace. In general, an iPredator is a person or group of persons who exploit, victimize, coerce, or stalk others through the use of computer technology in cyberspace. These offenders are identified through a variety of labels to include a child pornographer, an online sexual predator, a cyberstalker, a cyberbully, child exploiter, and child abuser. Unlike traditional predators of child abuse who often know their victims personally or abduct their victims for immediate victimization, the actions of these individuals are relational and are benefited through the exchange of information and communications over time and often over long distances as afforded by the online community.

Based upon information released by the US Census, over 95 percent of all citizens have access to the Internet;[10] thus, nearly three hundred million citizens are utilizing cyberspace. In considering the fact that young people in America, essentially all school-aged children have access to the Internet with the majority of these children (approximately 80 percent) having Internet access from the convenience of their home. This creates a large base of potential victims for perpetrators interested in the abuse of a child. Research suggests that patterns of computer usage are highest among the young with teenagers identified as one of the most likely age cohorts to access cyberspace on multiple occasions throughout the day.[11] Hence, a parent should expect that their child or teen is involved in Internet-based activities, to include not only information access for educational assignments, but also personal interactions with others in the virtual community through text messages or online social networks. However, not expected by parents are the online interactions that occur daily with strangers, which involve and are often initiated by their child, and may lead to abuse or victimization. In today's society, parents must acknowledge the risk cyberspace poses for their children.

Many parents are actively involved in the success of their children. As a parent, we teach our young children to speak, we teach them to walk, and we teach them to dress themselves. As our children enter school, we often devote our evenings to assisting with homework or as a spectator to a school play, a band concert, or another extracurricular event. In the teen years, we teach our children to drive and help them to plan for their adult lives. Ironically, in very few instances do parents ever discuss with their children the potential for their victimization within the online community and Internet safety. This absence of communications on the subject of ICAC only provides perpetrators an advantage in the exploitation and abuse of your child.

Without communications and instructions, few individuals learn. Reasons for this lack of communication on a subject that could alter the life of your child vary by parent and household. Again, for some parents,[12] their children are more skillful at using the online community than the parents; hence, they seek the children's advice on accessing information. With this request for assistance comes the assumption that since their children are skilled at utilizing the Internet, they are also skilled at avoiding individuals who are interested in harm. In these cases, parents do not consider the fact that their children could be a victim of an ICAC.

In other cases, parents assume that since their children are familiar with the Internet community then they are also familiar with the fact that there exist individuals in cyberspace with whom they should not communicate and should avoid. Finally, for some parents, their ignorance on the reach and capabilities of the Internet and cyberspace leads to a lack of knowledge regarding ICAC. As these parents are unaware of the potential dangers that exist for their children via the online community, they do not talk to their children about cyberspace safety.

Unfortunately, with many parents not aware of the volume of offensive information and sexual solicitations experienced by youth through cyberspace daily, they are not providing proactive measures to help their children avoid abuse. For many parents, the unexpected victimization of their children by an online perpetrator is never considered. Hopefully, as will become apparent to the readers of this book, parents should expect the potential victimization of their children through the online community and, with that expectation, plan for their children's protection.

As this chapter highlights what parents can normally expect as they enter the world of cyberspace, parents will be aware of the risks to their children. As this chapter provides discussions on the limitations for traditional "stay safe" strategies designed to protect children from abuse, parents will be better able to discuss ICAC with their children as well as the online terminology often utilized by their children and their potential abusers with the goal of child exploitation. Finally, as this chapter provides parents general strategies for introducing their children to cyberspace and safety, perhaps the potential victimization of their children is reduced or eliminated.

CYBERSPACE AND FRIENDS

Traditionally, the majority of the perpetrators of child abuse are family members or familia; however, this is not the case for ICAC. With cases of ICAC, the majority of the perpetrators are extrafamilial or someone outside of the family. Unfortunately, in most instances, the children or teens have been involved in many social interactions with their abuser via the online community prior to the abuse or exploitation. Thus, from the children's or teens' perspective, their abuser is not a stranger but someone they know.

Most children and teens, by nature, are trusting of adults and feel that, if they know someone then that person would not cause them harm. Hence, the mail carrier, who visits their home daily, is not a stranger. However, many children, who would not allow the mail carrier to enter their home when they are alone, would allow an online social contact (i.e., friend) to visit them via cell phone or computer camera without the supervision of their parent. To these children or teens, their online connection is not a stranger, but an individual welcomed into their lives and sometimes their home.

The term "stranger danger" has been used as a tool for the protection of our children from sexual victimization for decades. This phrase is reasonable for those offenders unknown to the child victims and the child's family or in protecting children from an individual outside of the family or the child's social network. However, many researchers have suggested that "stranger danger" has been one of the worst strategies ever incorporated into mainstream society to protect our children as, traditionally, in many of the sexual abuse cases, children are victimized by someone known to the child—not a stranger.[13] In fact, most individuals who are not familia but who sexually abuse children, are known to the family. Therefore, the strategy of stranger danger should be more appropriate for ICAC. However, with the close associations suggested through labels such as friend, connection, or group member, the identification of an online stranger is not always clear.

Generally with ICAC, extrafamilial abuse or abuse outside the family is common. Theoretically, stranger danger should be an excellent strategy to protect our children. Unfortunately, just as stranger danger does not deter the traditional cases of child sexual abuse, it also does not deter the majority of ICAC as in many cases, strangers are commonly identified in cyberspace by their child victims as *friends*.

In today's world of virtual reality, the reality is that the label of *friend* is often applied to a chatroom partner that the child or teen has met online but not face-to-face. In some cases, this friend may be a potential perpetrator of abuse in search of the next victim for child sexual exploitation. In these cases, this notion of familiarity among friends creates a welcoming environment for young victims. Hence, this notion of friendship is one of the most critical components in victimization in cyberspace and, in fact, facilitates the abuse.

Children and teens often model the behaviors of their parents. When they are young and want to grow up to be like us or write elementary school essays about us as their heroes, we love that imitation of our actions by our children. Unfortunately, they often imitate our everyday actions and interactions that may place them at risk for victimization in cyberspace.

As parents, we tell our young children not to talk to strangers yet we, as adults, converse daily with strangers in stores, banks, and so on, in clear view of our children. In other words, our children observe us doing exactly what we have told them not to do. In addition, we have socialized our children to be nice and polite to people and to interact with others in school, in church, and in play groups. Therefore, we should not be surprised when our teens utilize their skills of social interaction to be nice and polite and converse with individuals they do not really know within the online community. Thence, we have essentially told our children to "do as we say and not as we do." As a parent, we must be aware of the various ways in which we send mixed messages to our children about social interactions. Unthinkable by many parents is that our children may be placed (or place themselves) in harm's way because of the actions they have observed from us. Only by understanding the general concepts and terms of these ICAC as well as the processes involved with these types of victimizations may we protect our children. Hence, the Internet and the online community have produced unique challenges for parents wishing to protect their children in cyberspace.

INTERNET CRIME AND MY CHILD

Over two decades ago, during February 1996, President Bill Clinton signed the Telecommunications Reform Act,[14] which included regulatory reform and obscenity prohibitions to address the role of the Internet and Internet service providers (ISP). Within the Telecommunications Reform Act is the Communications Decency Act (CDA)—an attempt to censor the Internet of obscene, indecent, or annoying communications that are written or otherwise, as well as to prohibit the distribution of child pornography and imposed penalties for those individuals convicted of CDA violations.

In 2000 the Children's Internet Protection Act (CIPA)[15] was enacted by Congress to address concerns about children's access to obscene or harmful materials via the online community. The CIPA, through requirements on schools and libraries receiving educational discounts for Internet access, mandated that all schools and libraries adopt, implement, and provide proof of compliance to an Internet safety policy addressing the access of inappropriate matter by a minor, the safety and security of minors when using forms of electronic communication such as electronic mail and chat rooms, and the unauthorized disclosure, use, and dissemination of personal information. Hence, legislation has been enacted to help protect our children in cyberspace.

However, there are billions of people using the Internet every day and many of those users are under the age of eighteen. With the use of the Internet as a tool for criminal activity, and this increased use of the Internet, sexual crimes against children have increased and changed in terms of the dynamics associated with those crimes. In fact, research suggests that a large percentage of youth are approached in cyberspace for sexual exploitation daily. Although most of the sexual solicitations to young people fail, the quantity is such that many children and teens are still victims of many types of ICAC.

In cases of traditional, offline, sexual abuse, children between the ages of seven and thirteen have been identified as the most vulnerable. In cases of ICAC, although young children are potential victims, the primary vulnerability is with the teenager cohort as teens are the individuals most likely to be online. In addition, just as many cases of traditional child sexual abuse are not reported to law enforcement agencies, nearly 50 percent of the sexual solicitations of children or teens online are also not reported to law enforcement. Thus, just as with the offline (or traditional) cases of child sexual abuse, there are certainly more victims of child sexual abuse via the Internet than ever reported. In response, law enforcement agencies have begun to recognize the utility of the Internet and actions such as texting and sexting in the sexual abuse of children; however, few of these law enforcement agencies are providing specialized investigations in this area. Therefore, parents must take the lead.

WHO ARE THE PERPETRATORS
AND WHAT IS THEIR PROCESS?

In considering crimes against children, one must first consider the perpetrators and their process of abuse to understand the dynamics and outcomes of child sexual abuse. Specifically, in cases of child sexual abuse, a four-stage process or progression must occur before a child is abused. Those stages, or preconditions, are: (1) a motivation to sexually abuse a child by a perpetrator; (2) the overcoming of the perpetrator's internal inhibitors; (3) the overcoming of the external inhibitors; and (4) the overcoming of a child's resistance.[16] With ICAC, it is suggested that since many victims perceive their abusers as friends that overcoming a child's resistance is the easiest stage to satisfy.[17]

In traditional offline cases of child sexual abuse, the first stage is related to the identification of a motivated offender to sexually abuse a child. Parents should assume that these individuals will always exist. For some offenders, there exists a sexual attraction to the physical characteristics of children; however, these individuals will never act upon that attraction. In other cases, there exist individuals (child molesters) who will act upon their attraction to children if the opportunity is provided. For parents wishing to reduce their child's risk for online victimization, this first stage equates to not allowing their children or teens to communicate or interact with individuals unknown to the parents. However, this may not be an easy task for parents who are unaware of their children's actions in cyberspace.

The second phase of the sexual abuse of a child is overcoming the internal inhibitors within the perpetrator that would not allow the perpetrator to participate in the sexual abuse of a child. For some, it is the moral reasoning that child sexual abuse is wrong; for others it is the fear of detection. For most child molesters, the action is not unreasonable. In this stage, perpetrators must overcome their feelings of inappropriate actions. For some perpetrators, those inhibitors are often reduced or eliminated through the use of drugs and/or alcohol by the perpetrator. In addition, and as has been documented with most ICAC, the use of child pornography also reduces the perpetrator's perception that child sexual abuse is wrong. Thus, by viewing child pornography, the reality of child nudity and child sexuality is normalized.

The third stage is overcoming the external inhibitors which may deter child sexual abuse. For many children, the greatest external inhibitor is their parent. Those external inhibitors include the lack of supervision for the child or teen as well as the social support network for the child. Perpetrators of child sexual abuse know the significance in this stage of the process and, in response, often seek child victims of neglect. By targeting children (or teens) that are neglected or not supervised regularly as well as children who do not have adults for conversations or support, perpetrators are better able to select children for sexual abuse.

Finally, the last stage in the sexual abuse of children involves overcoming a child's resistance. Traditionally, children through a grooming process will become attached to their abuser to the point of affection and, in many cases, will allow the sexual abuse to continue in order that their abuser remain a part of their life. With ICAC, it is argued that this last stage is the easiest to overcome as, in many cases, the children or teens initiate the contact and continue the interactions with their abusers even after the abuse has occurred.

Four typologies of individuals who utilize the Internet to abuse children have been identified. These typologies are: (1) periodically prudent offenders; (2) fantasy-only offenders; (3) direct victimization offenders; and (4) commercial exploitation offenders.[18] Each of these typologies is distinct in its preferences and the motivational levels required to sexually exploiting children. First, the periodically prudent offender accesses images out of impulsivity or curiosity. These images are not necessarily only those of children and may include images of adults. Hence, this typology of offender is generally not the perpetrator of ICAC, but a consumer of child pornography if the opportunity or the pornography is provided. For these offenders, the intent is not toward children but rather toward pornography as these individuals, if involved with child pornography, usually do not utilize images of young children but rather children in their teens.

Second, fantasy-only offenders trade images to fuel their sexual interest in children; however, they do not have a history of actively abusing children.

This typology utilizes child pornography exclusively for their sexual excitement. These are the individuals commonly referred to as pedophiles as they do not abuse or molest children. However, on rare occasions, this typology of offender attempts to sexually abuse a child through molestation; therefore, these individuals become child molesters.

Third, direct victimization offenders use the online community to obtain child pornography for their own pleasure and to show to other children. As suggested in the title, these offenders are directly responsible for the victimization of children. If these individuals are not involved in the production of child pornography, then they are directly involved in the distribution of child pornography. This divulging of child pornography is a common mode for introducing pornography to children. This display of child pornography is directly related to the outcome of obtaining new child victims and indirectly as a means for grooming future victims. This typology will often be identified as the perpetrators of ICAC as well as the perpetrators of more traditional forms of child sexual abuse.

Finally, commercial exploitation offenders use the online community to assist in the production and distribution of child pornography for economic gain. This typology of offender is not sexually attracted to children, however, does view the child as a means of income. For this typology, the child is simply the product of consumption for those desiring sexual activities involving a child and a means of profit for the individual providing that child for consumption.

Other researchers have expanded the discussion on Internet users and their propensity toward child pornography as related to a variety of psychological pathways. These pathways, when satisfied, result in child sexual abuse. Those pathways include intimacy deficits, distorted sexual scripts, emotional deregulation, and antisocial cognitions. In other words, individuals who use the Internet to abuse children are often socially isolated or rejected, possess cognitive disorders which then misguide their sexual behaviors, have difficulties regulating their moods and emotions, and have general pro-criminal beliefs and actions.

Unfortunately for the law enforcement community and parents, offenders and offenses under the umbrella of ICAC are more diverse than in historical assessments of cases of child sexual abuse.[19] Specifically, offenders involved in ICAC are often younger than "traditional" child molesters and, based upon information provided through cases of ICAC, are both males and females. In fact, current research on ICAC suggests that crimes such as child pornography and cyberbullying are the result of peer-to-peer networks and that homemade images comprise a substantial proportion of the materials transmitted within the online community. In addition, sibling abuse, which has only recently been acknowledged as one of the most common forms of child sexual abuse, should not be discounted in the outcomes of ICAC, especially in cases of child pornography.

In general, in considering the demographics (age and gender) of the perpetrators of ICAC, those involved in the crimes of child solicitation, gross sexual imposition, sex rings, and sex tourism are usually adult males.[20] In the crimes of child pornography and sextortion, the perpetrators are generally male but are both youths and adults. In the ICAC of cyberbullying, cyberstalking, and sexting, the perpetrators are generally younger and are both males and females.[21] Finally, the perpetrators of severe forms of ICAC such as human trafficking are usually adult males but for cases involving very young children, the perpetrators may be both males and females. Thus, parents should be aware that, as cyberspace involves younger participants, which are both males and females, the perpetrators of many ICAC are also often young and both males and females.

Finally, research has suggested that viewing child pornography helps the pedophile to normalize the viewing of children as sexual objects. However, not all perpetrators of ICAC are the same and, while the majority of the perpetrators are motivated by a sexual attraction to children, some are motivated by profit. Therefore, cases of child sexual abuse and ICAC involve a variety of offenders such as sexual addicts, molesters, consumers of child pornography, child traffickers, and those involved in child sex rings.[22] To protect our children, parents must be aware of the role of cyberspace in not only their children's lives but also in the lives of perpetrators interested in the abuse of our children. Therefore, ICAC are very real and a potential risk to many of our children.

WILL MY CHILD BE A VICTIM?

Although any child may be a victim of sexual abuse, victims share some common characteristics. Specifically, research suggests that children who are victims of reported cases of sexual abuse are, in most cases, female.[23]

However, in the ICAC cases of child pornography and child sex rings, some research suggests that the victims are often male. In addition, in regard to victims of ICAC, research suggests that a distinction can be made between victims of sexual abuse and victims of child pornography as the first group includes victims exposed to online solicitations and most of the known victims of child pornography, although rarely identified, have not yet reached puberty. Finally, victims of child pornography tend to be female, use chat rooms, talk about sex online, and have often experienced physical or sexual abuse offline and generally at the hands of a family member.[24]

Parents wishing to protect their children from online sexual exploitation must not only understand the dynamics behind ICAC and the perpetrator, but must be aware of much of the common language used by individuals while communicating in cyberspace. The following is a list of twenty-five more common text abbreviations used in online conversations between victims and perpetrators. To help ensure the safety of our children, a parent should be aware of the meaning of these abbreviations and be aware of the implications of conversations where the abbreviations are utilized as many of these conversations indicate the desire for personal interactions and the concern for privacy by the child victims and their perpetrators.

Twenty-five Common Text and Chat Abbreviations[25]

CM	call me	PCM	please call me
DL	download	PRON	pornography
F2F	face to face	PRT	party
FBC	Facebook chat	PRW	parents are watching
H2CUS	hope to see you soon	PYT	pretty young thing
ILU	I love you	QTPI	cutie pie
IM	instant message	RYS	are you single?
IWALU	I will always love you	S2R	send to receive (i.e., send me your picture and I'll send you mine)
LGH	let's get high		
LH6	let's have sex	SYS	see you soon
LVM	left voice mail	TBL	text back later
O4U	only for you	TD2M	talk dirty to me
PAW	parents are watching	TMYL	tell me your location

In addition to the knowledge of terminology, parents should monitor their teens' cell phones and computers in an attempt to maintain their safety. If abbreviations such as these are observed, not only should parents talk to their children about online conversations, but also an investigation into all parties involved in these conversations should be initiated.

Over the last decade, more and more emphasis has been placed on the prevention of ICAC before they occur. While some individuals are critical about the money provided for prevention, statistics suggest that prevention efforts are largely successful. In addition, as with traditional cases of child sexual abuse, prevention is actually less expensive—financially and emotionally, than reactions after the victimization has occurred. By not only proactive efforts in the knowledge of these abbreviations, but also the reactive efforts of follow-up once these conversations are discovered, parents are in the best position to ensure the safety of their children.

HOW MIGHT I INTRODUCE
MY CHILD TO CYBERSPACE?

Studies on the perpetrators of ICAC are rare; therefore, efforts to protect children are usually based upon traditional forms of child sexual abuse and the risk factors involved in those cases. These efforts began in the 1960s with the identification of the Battered Child Syndrome and the parental and family characteristics that were associated with the outcome.[26] This prevention effort involved parenting classes as well as substance abuse treatment. In the late 1970s, when the public became aware of child sexual abuse, prevention programs to teach children to be cautious around individuals they do not know (i.e., stranger danger) were incorporated into the schools and community counseling programs.[27] With the 1974 Child Abuse Prevention and Treatment Act, federal funds were provided on multiple levels—federal, state, and local—to educate teachers and children on the subject of child abuse. Later, parents were added to the awareness and educational programs to prevent child abuse and the limited utility of one-shot programs was identified. Hence, today, prevention programs aimed at reducing child sexual abuse and, in particular, ICAC, now focus on the children, the parents, and the community with multiple avenues for information and resources. By communicating risks and then reminding children of these risks, parents may reduce the likelihood of their children becoming a victim of an ICAC.

However, it must be acknowledged that ICAC are, in many ways, different from traditional categories of child abuse. In particular, only about 10 percent of traditionally reported cases of child abuse are sexual abuse; however, the majority of the ICAC involve some aspect of sexual abuse. Also, in traditional cases of child sexual abuse or sexual exploitation, the majority of the victims have known their offenders prior to their victimization.[28] In cases of ICAC, the victims may have never met (face-to-face) their abuser until the abuse occurs. Also in traditional cases of child abuse, if the abuse is reported, it is reported immediately after the first assault. With ICAC, often victimization occurs on multiple occasions before it is reported, if reported at all. In addition, in traditional cases of child sexual abuse, African American children experience child sexual abuse at nearly twice the rate of Caucasian children and children from lower socioeconomic backgrounds at three times the rate of those children from more affluent backgrounds. With ICAC, children from all ethnic and social backgrounds are at risk. Finally, in traditional cases of child sexual abuse, those seeking to abuse children often seek quiet, shy, and passive children. With ICAC, the children or teens are likely to be actively involved in terms of initiating contacts and maintaining conversations with their abusers.[29]

SUMMARY

The parents' responsibility is the safety of their children. Today's world of children and cyberspace brings forth new challenges for parents when attempting to provide a secure environment for the protection of their children against ICAC. By being aware of the new dynamics associated with the online exploitation of children, and by introducing their children to the conditions of those dynamics, parents are better able to communicate messages of those dangers with their children.

Cases of ICAC often involve perpetrators who have been contacted by the victim, individuals who are younger than traditional child molesters, and individual who have been identified by the child as a friend. Finally, many types of ICAC involve child pornography and are often perpetrated by peers and not reported to law enforcement agencies. Hence, with these differences between traditional child abuse cases and ICAC, parents may be in the best position to protect their children from ICAC.

Chapter Three

Enticement, Sexual Imposition, Child Solicitation, and Child Pornography

Sarah has a daughter named Samantha who is a thirteen-year-old girl with a love of horses. Samantha's friend, Kellie, also loves horses and they began communicating via an online forum, then moved to instant messaging; however, they have never met in person. One evening Samantha comes to Sarah to ask if she would be able to meet Kellie at the mall to hang out for a few hours Friday evening. After reading the post, Sarah notices that Kellie has suggested that Samantha might not want to tell her mom.

Parents are aware that every day their children and teens participate in interactive online communications with their friends in cyberspace. What parents may not know is that these contacts or "friends" are, in some cases, individuals interested in the sexual abuse of their children. These are the perpetrators that continually search or review the Internet, chatrooms, and Facebook accounts for young people who post personal and potentially suggestive information as well as those young people, who spend much of their day online. Hence, perpetrators are seeking children and teens within cyberspace with a curiosity in sexual activity and who are without parental supervision.[1] Therefore, these children are the ideal targets and are at risk to become victims of child sexual abuse and sexual exploitation.

Child sexual abuse is a general term which includes, but is not limited to, the fondling of a child's genital, intercourse, rape, and the exploitation of children.[2] Traditional research supports the notion that most perpetrators of child sexual abuse are family members; however, as with most ICAC, this is not the case for these types of crimes. Child sexual exploitation is a type of sexual abuse to include child pornography and child prostitution in which children are victimized for not only sexual pleasure

31

but also for the money, power, or to elevate the status of another.[3] In cases such as these, the child or teen may not know all of their "clients"; however, they will know the person (or perpetrator) who has arranged and facilitated their victimization by another abuser.

The NCMEC collects information on cases of child abuse annually within the United States. Statistics from NCMEC on child abuse estimate that one in three females and one in six males will be sexually abused before age eighteen. In addition, one in five youths will be contacted within cyberspace for sex. This information is often shocking for parents as well as the public who perceive childhood as a time of joy and innocence. Of course, as with any estimates of victimization, this includes the cases where one child is victimized on multiple occasions. However, these estimates of sexual abuse have remained relatively consistent over the last few years with more cases receiving the attention of law enforcement and other criminal justice agencies. Unfortunately, as indicated by recent trends in abuse, with the incorporation of the Internet in our daily lives, more and more children and teens are being abused by an online contact every year.[4] In some cases, these individuals in contact with your child are interested in child pornography; in other cases, they are interested in sexual contact with your child. Regardless of the intent of these perpetrators, the sexual abuse of their children is often one of parents' worst fears.

This chapter focuses on the extrafamilial sexual abuse of children and, in particular, ICAC within cyberspace that involve enticement, sexual imposition, child solicitation, and child pornography. In particular, this chapter provides parents the definitions for these forms of ICAC, information on the legal responses to these criminal actions, and discussions on the perpetrators of these types of ICAC. In addition, this chapter provides parents information on recognizing signs of victimization in their children as well as suggestions for protecting their children while they are within cyberspace.

DEFINING TERMS

For clarity, child enticement is generally considered an action by an adult in attempting to entice or persuade a child into accompanying the adult for the purpose of sex.[5] As enticement involves initiating or coaxing a child into any vehicle, building, or secluded place for the intent of an unlawful sexual act; examples of enticement include asking a teen to meet them in a car outside a shopping mall, inviting a child to an adult's apartment without the permission or supervision of their guardian, or suggesting that a child meet them at their workplace after the business is closed and the building is empty. At one time, these invitations were offered in person, through a child's peer, or through a telephone call. Today, these invitations are offered within cyberspace, through the Internet or a cell phone. For parents who have often worried about their children's peers enticing them into illegal activities such as underage drinking, this is an additional concern.

Sexual imposition (or gross sexual imposition) occurs when a perpetrator forces two individuals to engage in sexual contact without consent or free will.[6] Gross sexual imposition also includes the sexual abuse of victims under the age of thirteen and victims without the intellectual ability to provide consent. For clarity, from a legal definition, a child, because of age (i.e., under eighteen), may not provide consent to sexual activity.

The action of sexual imposition is an illegal action which is prohibited by state laws and includes actions that are offensive to the victim or that cause two or more individuals to participate in sexual relations through force or coercion. The phrase sexual imposition is generally restricted to victims between the age of thirteen and fifteen. Gross sexual imposition involves the use of drugs or alcohol to force or coerce young victims into sexual contact with a perpetrator or a third party.[7] Examples of gross sexual imposition include drugging a fourteen-year-old girl to persuade her into the actions of exotic dancing or prostitution and providing alcohol to two twelve-year-old children to force them into participating in oral sex with each other.

Child solicitation is an attempt to lure a child into sexual activity with an adult and often involves an exchange of money or property for sex.[8] These sexual activities may include any sexual act from fondling to sexual intercourse. Technically, electronic solicitation refers to the action by an adult in an attempt to seduce or persuade a person, under the age of sixteen, into participating in a sexual act by means of a computer or cellular device. Hence, electronic solicitations occur in cyberspace.

In some states, the sexual solicitation of a child involves children under the age of sixteen, in some states under the age of eighteen. Finally, in some states the age of the offender and victim is critical (i.e., eighteen and thirteen, respectively) in determining cases of child solicitation as cases involving peers of similar ages are rarely prosecuted. Examples of child solicitation include asking a child to perform oral sex with an adult in exchange for a shopping trip to the mall, asking a child to participate in sex in exchange for the newest computer play station, and asking a child to participate in sex for money. For the purpose of this chapter, the solicitation of a minor and electronic solicitation will both be referred to as child solicitation and both will involve the sexual abuse of a child younger than eighteen. Hence, child solicitation is a concern for parents.

Finally, child pornography is defined as a photo, film, or other visual representation of a person under the age of eighteen engaged in sexual activity or a photo, film, or other visual representation of the genitalia of a person under the age of eighteen. In cases of child pornography, force is not an issue as many teens are willing to send homemade images of a sexual nature to others. Unfortunately, if these homemade images are of nude or seminude teens and are present on the cell phone of a teen, and if the images are of individuals under the age of eighteen, then these images may be considered child pornography.

Child pornography is the most common ICAC today as the majority of individuals, involved in any type of ICAC, are also most often in possession of child pornography. Each of the illegal activities discussed within this chapter are common in today's virtual world. Each of these illegal activities involves children and each of these illegal activities should be of concern for parents who are attempting to protect their children from ICAC.

WHY ARE ICAC SUCH A PROBLEM?

The computer and cyberspace provide individuals of all ages the opportunity to interact. Hence, the Internet has become essential in our day-to-day activities of work, entertainment, information gathering, and socializing. Unfortunately, some of those interactions are not in the best interest of a child. Cyberspace provides individuals wishing to contact a child for victimization the opportunity of introduction. Hence, these perpetrators, who would not normally be able to contact a particular child, now have that ability. It is those individuals who should be of concern for parents wishing to protect their children from ICAC and, as a parent of a child utilizing cyberspace, it is those individuals whom we must identify.

Teenagers, as most parents soon realize, may look and speak like adults, but they are still children. Research suggests that during the teen years, the part of the brain responsible for reasoning and controlling emotions has not completely developed. Hence, teens often lack the rational decision-making process required for their safety and protection.[9] For those teens, who seek online conversations and sometimes adult conversations, online predators are eager to engage them in conversation and eventually eager to engage them in sexual activities.

Child molesters approach teens and young children in cyberspace for many purposes including sexual conversations, sexual activities, and to obtain child pornography. These abusers, skilled at initiating conversations and interactions with children, use a variety of strategies to engage their targets in sexual conduct to include initiating conversations about sports, animals, the environment, or even the unfairness of their parents. Hence, perpetrators of child sexual abuse are often very skilled at attracting and maintaining the interest of children and now the Internet is a tool for success for these individuals who wish to prey on young victims.[10] As sexual predators access social networks to identify children, chat lines to interact with those children, and social networks to communicate with other adults who share their same fantasies of child sexual abuse, the Internet and cyberspace may potentially be one of the most dangerous environments for children.

WHAT ARE THE LEGAL RESPONSES?

There are thousands of websites for chatting (or chatrooms) that advocate for adult–child sexual relations in operation every day. The most commonly known of these groups is the North American Man/Boy Love Association (NAMBLA) which is an organization established in the late 1970s with its mission to remove Age of Consent Laws as related to sexual activities.[11] As pressures from the public and law enforcement have increased, this group has essentially dwindled to only a few publicly known members and now operates largely within the online community or cyberspace.

Parents must acknowledge the harm these individuals intend to inflict upon their children. In addition, parents should also be aware that, through the anonymity of such websites, predators can, in some cases, pretend to be the same age as the child or teen and therefore establish a bond as a peer to the child while they provide false information about themselves or their interests. Using this tactic, perpetrators are often able to convince the child or teen to send them sexual text messages (sexting), nude or semi-nude pictures, or even meet with them in person. Of course, all of these actions eventually result in child victimization.

However, not all adult-to-child sexual encounters initiated in cyber-space require deception. In fact, the majority of the cases of youth victims will meet willingly with their abusers even when these young people know that the encounter will be sexual in nature. In addition, recent re-search on ICAC suggests that in at least 50 percent of the cases of child sexual abuse, the child (or teen) initiated the contact with their abuser and was concerned about the age of their perpetrator.[12] Hence, the notion of "stranger danger" does not apply to these types of ICAC as threats or deception by abusers are less likely to occur than originally thought and child victims are willing to participate in the first sexual encounter with these predators. In other cases, offenders are not dishonest and may reveal to the child their age, while still befriending the child through flat-tery and expressed mutual interest in whatever will enhance their bond. In these cases, the child is attracted to the feelings of being "special" and "mature" that are provided by the abuser and just as in traditional cases of child sexual abuse, the child will continue with their sexual activities to maintain a connection with their perpetrator; hence, the victimization of the child is likely to occur.

Also, in some cases, offenders may openly solicit a child to engage in sexual conduct and make an arrangement to meet with them. In fact, it is suggested that many child or teen victims of these types of ICAC perceive that they are involved in a relationship with their abuser.[13] This may occur even in cases where the child, through their Internet chat with the abuser, has revealed that the teen is under the legal age to consent to having sex; however, the teen perceives themselves as grown up and their perpetrator does not disagree.

Finally, one cannot eliminate the fact that sometimes family members are involved in ICAC. These fathers, mothers, or siblings—motivated by an immediate need for money—may choose the sexual exploitation of their child or sibling through the online community as a necessary action to address their financial crisis.

To address the issue of child abuse and computer technology, the 1977 Sexual Exploitation of Children Act prohibited the transportation of child pornography by mail or the computer.[14] In 1984, for clarity of definitions, the Child Protection Act defined anyone younger than eighteen as a child.[15] In 1988, the Child Protection Enforcement Act made it unlawful to use a computer to transport child pornography and provided a specific age definition of a child based upon the physical characteristics of the child. In 1994, the Jacob Wetterling Act provided the first legislative initiative to establish as sex offender registry.[16] In 1996, Megan's Law amended the Wetterling Act to include a community notification system to the registry to alert the public when a convicted sex offender is released from prison and moves into their area.[17] Unfortunately, with ICAC, the residential location of the sex offender is not significant within an online community. In response, and also in 1996, President Bill Clinton signed the Telecommunications Reform Act, which included regulatory reform and obscenity prohibitions. Within the Telecommunications Reform Act is the Communications Decency Act (CDA),[18] which is an attempt to censor the Internet of obscene, indecent, or annoying communications written or otherwise, and imposes penalties on those convicted of CDA violations. In 2000, the Wetterling Act was again amended to the Campus Sex Crimes Protection Act[19] to require that convicted sex offenders who wish to enroll in institutions of higher education must submit their criminal records to the college or university.

In 2010, the Child Abuse, Prevention, and Treatment Act was reauthorized and continues to be recognized as the largest body of legislation intended to protect children. In 2014, the child victims' and child witnesses' rights act allows victims of child abuse to provide their testimonies via videos.

International efforts to address these types of ICAC include Interpol's International Child Sexual Exploitation Image database, which is available to specialized investigators in a variety of countries. This database uses image comparison software to connect victims and locations.[20] As of 2016, there were approximately fifty countries connected to the database. Since its inception in 2001, approximately ten thousand child victims have been identified and removed from harm and approximately five thousand perpetrators have been identified to law enforcement or the courts. However, not all of the convictions for child sexual abuse within the online community are upheld globally or in the United States as demonstrated by the following two US examples.

In May of 2015, the Texas Criminal Court of Appeals removed names from sex offender registries and set aside felony convictions for several individuals convicted of child imposition.[21]

In August of 2016, the Minnesota Appeals Court overturned a conviction of child solicitation as the child victim claimed in cyberspace that she was 16 and not her actual age of 14.[22]

Unfortunately, and again, without the jurisdictional limits of the online community, the enforceability of these laws is nearly impossible. Cyberspace is a global community without regional boundaries and the technology used to support cyberspace changes quickly. There are over one billion online users every day in cyberspace. In addition, research suggests that teen victims rarely provide clear accounts of their sexual abuse to law enforcement. Hence, parents must be informed on the subjects of ICAC to protect their children within cyberspace.

WHO ARE THESE PERPETRATORS?

Current research suggests that perpetrators involved in child enticement, child solicitation, and sexual imposition are usually adults with the desire for sexual activity with individuals considered too young to provide consent. For many, these individuals are referred to as pedophiles. By clinical definition, pedophiles are sexually attracted to the physical characteristics of a child; however, by legal definition, child molesters are those individuals who act upon that desire for sexual activity with a child. However, it should be noted that predators, who utilize sexual solicitations, were nearly twice as likely to target females.

In considering child pornography, research suggests that it is not always the result of an adult-child interaction and that often child pornography is the result of peer-to-peer networks and those peers are the same age. In fact, one out of ten teens admits to sharing nude pictures of themselves online with few believing that their "friends" will share (or forward) their pictures to or with others.[23] With today's cell phones, homemade images, or those images that are not commercially produced, comprise a substantial proportion of the large volume of child pornography viewed and available online. In fact, the NCMEC reported that over one million tips related to child pornography were received in 2014 alone. Today, the offenders involved in the activities of child pornography via the Internet are usually younger than most offenders of traditional incidents of child sexual abuse and, in many cases, the original image of child pornography was from the teen's own cell phone and was often not solicited.

Traditionally, the majority of the perpetrators of child sexual abuse are within the family. With ICAC, some of the perpetrators, or at least those perpetrators arranging the victimization of the child, are family members. However, in the majority of the ICAC, the perpetrators are from outside the family.[24]

In addition to child molesters, some perpetrators are identified as sexual addicts or a person who is preoccupied with the thought of sex and plans their actions with the ultimate goal of sexual release.[25] In these cases, the child is the means for the release.

Finally, in addition to those with a sexual attraction to children or an addiction to sex, other perpetrators are involved in the sexual abuse or sexual exploitation of children as a means of profit. In crimes such as enticement, sexual imposition, child solicitation, and child pornography, some of the perpetrators (especially those involved in child pornography) choose child abuse for profit. However, the majority of ICAC perpetrators abuse children as a result of a sexual attraction to children and not for financial gain. However, there are those researchers who suggest that, just as child trafficking is extremely profitable, so is the potential profit for distributing child pornography in cyberspace.

As stated previously, perpetrators who utilize the Internet for the ICAC of child enticement, sexual imposition, child solicitation, or child pornography are usually classified into four categories: (1) periodically prudent offenders, (2) fantasy-only offenders, (3) direct victimization offenders, and (4) commercial exploitation offenders.[26]

Periodically prudent offenders will access images out of impulsivity or curiosity with the images not exclusively children. This typology of offender is generally not the perpetrator of an ICAC and is not involved in child enticement, imposition, or child solicitation. However, these are the offenders (as well as the next category of offenders) who seek pornography via the online community for personal sexual gratification. These are the individuals who have viewed not only adult pornography, but also may have viewed some of the twenty-eight million images of child pornography analyzed through the US Child Victim Identification Program in 2014.[27]

Fantasy-only offenders trade images to fuel their sexual interest in children; however, they do not have a history of actively sexually abusing children. These individuals, although they may possess child pornography, are not the individuals who are online seeking children to meet and sexually abuse. These individuals seek online images (often homemade) of young people in sexually provocative pictures and, with teens sharing images of themselves, there is no limit to the images available. This typology also utilizes the child pornography for their own sexual excitement,[28] however, rarely (if ever) attempts to sexually abuse a child through molestation.

Direct victimization offenders use the online community as a source for child pornography and then utilize the child pornography as a tool to assist in the grooming of future victims.[29] As nearly 10 percent of youth report unsolicited exposure to distressing sexual materials via the online community, and with predators actively seeking young people who appear to welcome enticement from adults, this category of abusers not only has an abundance of child sexual material, but also an abundance of perceived willing-to-participate teen victims. This typology of child molester will often be reported to law enforcement by parents as the perpetrators of child solicitation as well as perpetrator of other types of ICAC.

Finally, commercial exploitation offenders utilize the online community to assist in the production and distribution of child pornography for economic gain.[30] This category of perpetrator sees the child as simply the product for consumption and is a concern for many individuals interested in preventing ICAC. These perpetrators browse ads for child sexual encounters as well as child pornography through online classified ad sites such as Craig's List, Backpage, Cityvibe, myRedBook, Eros, and

Es-courts. For many of these perpetrators, they themselves may not be attracted to the physical characteristics of a child at all; however, their customers are in the market for either child pornography or a child to sexually abuse and these perpetrators attempt to capitalize on that market. Hence, parents should acknowledge that not all of the perpetrators of ICAC are the same and, while most are motivated by a sexual attraction to children, some are motivated by profit. Regardless of the motivations or demographics of perpetrators, children are the victims of these types of ICAC.

IS MY CHILD A PERPETRATOR?

In addition to blurring the boundaries of victimization and social convention, one of the most popular discussions of ICAC concerns the relationship between victim and offender. Researchers suggest that peers often request more child pornography than strangers and that peers are often likely to provide nude or partially nude pictures of themselves to their peers. In addition, child pornography, posted on the Internet is used to justify the acceptability of adult and teen sexual relationships and is utilized by adult and teen perpetrators to assure victims of the normality of their requests for pornography. In 2008, Interpol identified over five hundred thousand online images and approximately seven hundred victims of child pornography.[31] Five years later, Interpol identified over one million online images of child pornography with victims of child pornography that were not only similar in gender and age to traditional child victims of sexual abuse but also included both males and females of all ages.

Traditionally, child pornography was produced and distributed through the work of pornographic groups or sex rings and adults who work together to exploit children for sex; this is not the case today.[32] The Internet and the online community have changed the technical mode for child pornography and sexual solicitations and, in some cases, have changed the roles of teens from exclusively a victim role to a victim or offender role.

Teens involved in either the viewing or creation of child pornography often display behavioral indicators similar to victims of child abuse. Specifically, children involved in the production of child pornography may appear withdrawn, depressed, and often are dishonest about their computer usage.[33] In addition, the child or teen involved in the viewing of child pornography may notice the bodies of others and show a tolerance for previously ignored sexually graphic movies.

Finally, teens involved in the viewing of child pornography (as is often the case in viewing adult pornography) will begin spending time out of the home and in restaurants or cafes with Internet access.[34] Specifically, the children or teens will begin locking their door when using the computer in their room, turning the computer off or switching sites when someone enters the room while they are on the computer, and will often delete their search histories. Finally, it is not unusual for victims of child pornography to use others' accounts (usually their abuser's account) for online calls and merchandise or for those involved in the production of child pornography to have money in excess of what they have been given by their parents or earned through their after-school job. This availability of additional money should also be an indicator of a teen's involvement in ICAC.

Parents must be aware that with improved technology and more exhibitionism sites, the use of the Internet has increased and the cases of child pornography have multiplied. For many victims, the statement "once it is on the Internet, it is there forever" is true.

IS MY CHILD A VICTIM?

Often a child victim of sexual abuse will provide hints of that abuse through behavioral indicators instead of the physical indicators of pain, bruises, sexually transmitted diseases, or urinary tract infections. These child victims may experience problems in school, problems with authority, be comfortable with the use of sexual language or descriptions of sexual acts, and either be extremely aggressive or extremely submissive in their interactions with peers. Parents should be aware that in cases of child exploitation through enticement, solicitation, and child pornography many children will display behavioral indicators similar to traditional victims of sexual abuse. Just as a victim of traditional child sexual abuse, child victims of ICAC are often withdrawn from their family and friends. In addition, these child victims spend such of their time online and alone. Finally, victims of these types of ICAC are often secretive about their communications and will often have many phone numbers in the cell phone's contact list with new numbers being added on a regular basis.[35]

HOW DO I PROTECT MY CHILD?

As with all categories of ICAC, supervision and communication at a very young age are essential for protecting our children. Parents should explain to their children throughout all stages of their development that individuals attempting to elicit a conversation with them while within the online community may or may not have their best interests in mind. In addition, parents should be mindful of the behavioral indicators of victims of ICAC.

Just as traditionally we have taught our children to beware of strangers attempting to approach them or talk to them, we must now caution our children about online approaches. Friends who attempt to converse with our children within the online community without parental consent and in particular, friends from the online community who attempt to meet our children are to be avoided and are not really friends to children.

Child enticement, sexual imposition, child solicitation, and child pornography are just some of the ICAC that exist today. Parents must be aware of these crimes against our children. As parents begin conversations with their children at an early age, and continue these conversations throughout the teen years, parents are better able to protect their children and our children are better able to protect themselves from these forms of ICAC.

SUMMARY

Along with the growth of cyberspace comes the growth of child exploitation. Four types of these ICAC are enticement, sexual imposition, child solicitation, and child pornography. Each of these crimes involves children and has the propensity to create long-term consequences of a negative nature for the victims. Unfortunately, with the exception of child pornography, parents are usually not aware of these crimes and the risk that cyberspace provides in facilitating these crimes. Child enticement is an action by an adult of attempting to entice or persuade a child into accompanying him or her for the purpose of sex. Sexual imposition occurs when a perpetrator forces two individuals to engage in sexual contact without consent or free will. Finally, child solicitation involves luring a child into sexual activity with an adult and often involves an exchange of money or property for sex.

Research suggests that perpetrators involved in child enticement, child solicitation, and sexual imposition are usually adults with the desire for sexual activity with individuals considered too young to provide consent. Currently, those perpetrators involved in child pornography may be adults or teen peers. Regardless of the perpetrators, parents should be aware of these crimes as related to the victimization of their child.

Many victims of these types of ICAC experience problems in school, problems with authority. They are often uncomfortable with individuals in positions of authority while, at the same time, very comfortable with the use of sexual language or descriptions of sexual acts. In addition, many victims of these ICAC are either extremely aggressive or extremely submissive in their interactions with others. In some cases, with these ICAC, victims perceive that they are actually involved in a relationship with their abuser. Finally, some victims of these types of crimes experience physical symptoms such as sexually transmitted diseases or urinary tract infections as a result of their victimizations.

As with all categories of ICAC, supervision, communication, and monitoring at a very young age are essential for protecting our children. Parents must explain to their children throughout all stages of their development that individuals attempting to elicit a conversation with them while within the online community may not have their best interests in mind.

Chapter Four

Sexting and Sextortion

Lindsey is a seventeen-year-old girl with a twenty-year-old boyfriend. Lately, she has been spending a lot of time alone and in her room with the door locked. One evening, her father asks her why the door is always locked and Lindsey replies that she likes her privacy. One week later, Lindsey attempts to overdose with sleeping pills. She later confesses to her father that her "boyfriend" has been demanding that she send him pictures of her engaged in sex acts with their family dog.

Cyberspace and cell phone technology allow communications to occur throughout the world and from a variety of locations. For most individuals, the ability to connect to another person from the convenience of their car, while walking in the park or while sitting in a movie theater, is one of the best rewards for living in our age of technology. Children and teens also enjoy these opportunities. In reality, children and teens, through cyberspace and their cell phones, may connect to anyone at any time and without the permission of their parents. Should parents really be surprised when their children connect to individuals that they would perceive as inappropriate?

For teens and preteens, the primary threat for victimization is not "stranger danger" but themselves.[1] In today's world of technology and cell phone availability, teens are now more at risk of victimization from their own initiated interactions with individuals in cyberspace. Parents, who usually provide cell phones to their children, have no idea with whom their children are interacting. We want our children to have a cell phone in case of an emergency and will pay the expenses associated with that cell phone to help ensure our children's safety. Unfortunately, what most parents do not realize is that the very tool we have purchased to help our children stay safe is the tool that can facilitate their victimization. Two of the more common actions that involve a cell phone and are related to ICAC are sexting and sextortion.[2]

A victim-precipitated crime is a crime in which the victim's behavior was the initial action (directly or indirectly) that led to their victimization and the illegal behavior. In 2000 when Congress enacted the Children's Internet Protection Act (CIPA) as an attempt to limit a child's exposure to obscene or harmful content received via the Internet, the notion of children precipitating their own victimization was not considered.[3] With today's abundance of cell phones, a child's participation in their own victimization is now being realized. Unfortunately, as teens or preteens are often the ones initiating contact with individuals who will expose them to those obscene materials, the CIPA restrictions are less likely to be enforced in many cases of these ICAC. Hence, in most cases, it is the parents who will protect their child from victimization via cell phone usage.

This chapter focuses on the extrafamilial sexual abuse of children and the ICAC involving sexting and sextortion, as related to peers and perpetrators. In addition, this chapter provides a discussion on the conditions that often exist prior to sexting and prior to sextortion as well as legal efforts to reduce a teen's involvement in these types of ICAC. Finally, this chapter provides information to parents in terms of strategies for protecting their children from the dangerous outcomes of sexting and sextortion.

To begin the discussion, first the distinction between texting and sexting must be acknowledged. Today's cell phones have the capabilities to send and receive text messages. Individuals may converse without saying a word. Texting is not sexting; however, sexting is a type of texting. As suggested in current research, sexting has increased in rank in terms of parental concerns; in 2016 sexting was identified as the sixth biggest worry for parents, an increase from thirteenth in 2015. For clarity, sexting is defined as the sending or receiving sexually suggestive images or messages through a cell phone.[4] In these cases of sexting, there are multiple contacts (sexts) between parties; hence, the term sexting assumes the existence of repeated messages or images of a sexual nature. For adults (i.e., those ages eighteen or older), sexting is not illegal and is common practice in young adults throughout the dating stages of a relationship. However, for those under the age of eighteen, sexting is illegal as it involves the sending of explicit sexual images or messages, which are considered forms of child pornography. In other words, as the images and messages are of and from individuals under the age of eighteen, they are considered illegal.

Sextortion is a severe negative outcome and a result of sexting. For clarity, sextortion is defined as a form of sexual abuse where an abuser threatens to reveal sexually explicit images of a victim (sent unsolicited by the teen victim) unless that particular victim meets the specific demands of the perpetrator.[5] These demands include providing more sexually graphic images or videos. Simply stated, sextortion is a form of blackmail in which images are used to force individuals (most likely teens) into performing sexual favors or actions to prevent the release of those images to their friends, family, and the online community. Both of these activities occur in today's virtual cyberspace and both are becoming more common forms of teen or child sexual exploitation.

Statistics indicate that approximately 95 percent of all teenagers within the United States have their own cell phones and that those teens send text messages.[6] As parents will attest, in most cases they are more likely to receive a text from their children than a phone call. In some cases, those teen text messages become teen sext messages. Again, sexting is vaguely defined to include the sending or receiving of sexual images or language on a repeated basis; however, most state laws generally focus only on the nude or seminude images of minors sent or received through sext messages. Unfortunately, these images, often circulated to many within the online community, have the propensity to exist forever. Hence, the victimization of those pictured in the images, usually the teen, is considered never-ending and never in the past.

WHY DOES MY TEEN SEXT?

Parents should understand that sexting, just as alcohol and marijuana use by teens three decades ago, is often the result of peer pressure to "fit in" with today's teen social groups. If their peers were not sexting, then their teen would probably not be sexting.[7] Sexting occurs and, in many cases, their teen is an active participant.

Teenagers will sext for a variety of reasons. For some teens, sexting is viewed as "normal" behavior or simply as a mode for flirtation. As our society equates sexual activity with dating relationships and, as our teens are now experiencing the newness of relationships, sexual activities involving their standard form of communications (i.e., their cell phones) seem natural and acceptable. Teens today prefer the ease of texting, in many cases, over face-to-face conversations.[8] A picture of themselves nude or partially nude as well as sexual language communicated via their cell phone is expected. In addition, sexting is often viewed as cool or something that the popular kids would do and it is not normally viewed as a negative action.

For many teens within the school setting, the existence of the clique structure is the primary means of socialization.[9] These cliques, which, often are based upon inequality, involve groups such as jocks and cheerleaders (the cool cliques) and geeks and loners (the uncool cliques). If the cool clique is participating in sexting, and many are, then this has an enormous impact on others, both within and outside of that clique. The notion that if the "cool kids sext, then I should also sext" is impressed upon those teens within that environment. For many of the teens, sexting allows them some equality with the popular groups in the school; hence, they are participating in sexting.

Research suggests that, in addition, females are less likely to perceive the sexting of nude pictures of themselves as illegal.[10] In many cases, females will often sext for social attention or from a request from a male. As a result of the sexting, females receive the positive attention that they desire and even may result in them being perceived as sexy, hot, or even beautiful. Males will sext from peer pressure as their friends also send pictures of their groin areas or "dick pics" to others. Hence, in the teen male social setting, just as the case for teen males participating in delinquent activities, teen males are more likely to sext if they are encouraged to do so by their peers and are less likely to sext without the encouragement of others. Unfortunately, sexting cases are largely unrecognized by the media as a threat to child safety; therefore, parents and teens are often unaware of the consequences.

Finally, from a parental-protection perspective, it is difficult to convince our children not to sext when Hollywood enforces the rewards of fame and fortune for those who sext explicit pornographic images to all. Reality shows and YouTube videos have made ordinary people famous for participating in sometimes unique and sexual activities on a public level. As a parent, we warn our children about the negative outcomes of sexting, yet media highlights individuals who have participated in the very activities we are attempting to prohibit. As expected, from our child's perspective individuals who sext are often wealthy and perceived as popular by the mainstream media.

HOW DOES THE LAW PROTECT MY CHILD?

Research suggests that 50 percent of teen males and 30 percent of teen females have received sexual messages or images.[11] In addition, approximately 20 percent of all teens admit to having sexted suggestive messages or images.[12] Finally, teens that pay the expenses related to the ownership of their cell phone (i.e., phone, data usage plan) are more likely to participate in sexting. However, the actions of these teens are illegal and, regardless of the source, the materials distributed are still considered child pornography. Thus even if a teen sexts an image of their own body, they have technically produced and distributed child pornography.

Approximately twenty states have incorporated sexting terminology into their child protection laws with nine states actually defining the word *sexting*.[13] Finally depending upon the circumstances of the images, sexting may also be a crime under federal law. In addition, the federal Prosecutional Remedies and Other Tools to end the Exploitation of Children Today (PROTECT) Act of 2003 states that it is illegal to produce, distribute, receive, or possess with intent to distribute any obscene visual depiction of a minor engaging in sexually explicit conduct.[14] Hence, it is illegal for children and teens to participate in sexting. States without specific legislation may allow the addition of federal charges for those arrested for sexting with a minor or sextortion. However, due to the 1938 Federal Juvenile Delinquent Act, which called for separate adult and juvenile courts, it is rare that a teen (or anyone under the age of eighteen) perpetrator will be prosecuted for sexting or sextortion. Unfortunately, what this equates to is that some children may be victims of child pornography via sexting without a child predator being punished.

Generally, laws are thought to be seen as a deterrence for an action. However, there has been no research to suggest that, even if teens are aware of the legal penalties for sexting, they will be less likely to participate. In fact, just as with other status offenses such as underage drinking, some research suggests that teens were slightly more likely to participate in sexting when they are aware of potential serious legal consequences. For some teens, just as with participating in the vandalism of property, the excitement of being involved in an activity with the potential outcome of being arrested is desired. Unfortunately, sexting can lead to sexual harassment and facilitates actions of revenge or retaliation in negative relationships.

Penalties for convictions for sexting vary for adults and juveniles.[15] The penalties for adults convicted of sexting with a teen include up to five years of incarceration, fines, probation, and entry of their name and information on the national Sex Offender Registry. Penalties for juveniles include warnings, fines, community service, counseling, probation, and detention to include home confinement or residence in a group home. Of course, prior to the investigation, prosecution, and conviction, reporting (which does not occur at the teen level) is necessary.

As an indicator for the potential popularity for sexting, in 2004, approximately 65 percent of teens had their own cell phone. In 2008 approximately 80 percent of teens had their own cell phone; in 2015 approximately 95 percent of teens had their own cell phones. Hence, with more teens using cell phones, with teens often aware of the legal penalties for sexting, and with sexting cases included in what criminologists call the "dark figure," or unreported crime, it is not unexpected that cases of sexting are not only continuing in the teen world, but also increasing in cyberspace.

IS MY CHILD THE VICTIM OR THE PERPETRATOR?

As stated, children and teens are involved in sexting for a variety of reasons. For the most part, older teens are more likely to sext when compared to preteens. However, children as young as ten have been known to not only receive but also voluntarily send messages or images of a sexual nature.[16] For parents, this is difficult to accept. Just as teen sexual activity is a subject of taboo in the household, so is the subject of sexting. Unfortunately, parents, unaware of the practice of sexting in the teen community, are not likely to be the first individuals to recognize their child's or teen's involvement in sexting. Thus, parents are not likely to initiate conversations on the dangers of sexting.

For most teens, the thought of their peers involved in sexting is not something that they would consider inappropriate or surprising. Again, reasons for teen involvement in sexting mirror the reasons provided by adults for the same action. They are involved in a sexual relationship and want to provide their partner a nice "surprise" during the day. They are involved in a relationship but are unable to see their partner so they communicate and fulfill their desire for a sexual release through sexting. Finally, they are interested in a new partner and want to provide that newly desired person a sexual conversation or image as a flirtation. Hence, the teen is the perpetrator of sexting and sexting is a normal part of a relationship between two people.

Other more specific reasons for teens sexting also help to explain teen involvement in sexting. Specifically, teens might sext if they are interested in a person but are not currently sexually active.[17] Sexting provides the teens an opportunity for a sexual relationship without the loss of their virginity. Other teens may participate in sexting because they prefer communications within the online community instead of face-to-face conversations. This is especially true for females as research suggests that many young women perceive the cell phone and sexting as a very useful form of communication across geographic distances. These teens are often extremely shy in conversations with persons of interest or worried about saying something wrong. By sexting teens can review their conversation before it is sent and, therefore, be more confident in their part of the social interactions.

Solicitations of compliments are also a reason for teen sexting.[18] With teens, mass media representations of the perfect human body place enormous pressures on young women and men in terms of physical appearance. Females, who may be proud of their body or their appearance in certain sexually suggestive clothing, may sext others as an attempt to receive attention or compliments regarding their appearance. Males, with the pressure to have a large erected penis, may sext pictures of their genitalia as an attempt to display their ability to be a manly or virile lover (if given the opportunity). Again, in these cases, both male and female teens are the perpetrators for distributing child pornography.

In addition, there is also an importance in gender as related to sexting. Even as gender inequality has diminished, in the teen world, sexism still exists. Perhaps in the most general of notions, it is asserted that girls' and young women's bodies are somehow the property of boys and young men. One of the most common practices in teen sexting is a male will solicit and the female will comply. Hence, images of the female's body are distributed to both male and female perpetrators of sexting.

Finally, teens involve themselves in delinquent behaviors because of boredom.[19] Teens are also involved in sexting in many cases simply because of opportunity. The teen, in search of activities for the day and with parents, often at a disadvantage with password-protected access to cyberspace, will participate in sexting with another or others to have something to do.

Thus, for parents, the question of whether their child or teen is the victim or perpetrator of sexting is often answered with—yes, to both. Teens and preteens, because of their willingness in many cases to send sexually explicit narratives or images, may later discover that their private "message" is now public. The teen initiator (or perpetrator) is now the victim of sexting.

SEXTING TO SEXTORTION

Teens who have participated in sexting place themselves at risk for other forms of child sexual exploitation. Specifically, many teens who have sexted messages to one certain individual may later discover that their "private" image or message has now been viewed by hundreds of individuals within the virtual community. These individuals are now victims of child pornography or sometimes even victims of sextortion, simply from their own initiated and distributed image.

> In 2015, a 31-year-old former Top Gun Navy Instructor and veteran of Iraq, living in Virginia, was convicted of posing as a teenager on the Internet, and extorted (sextortion) young girls into sending him sexually graphic photos of themselves and each other.[20]

> In 2016, a 25-year-old Baton Rouge, Louisiana male was convicted of extortion (sextortion) as he had obtained compromising pictures of multiple child victims then received even more graphic images as a result of his threats to release the original images to friends and family.[21]

Sextortion involves the use of threats to expose sexual images of the victim in order to make the victim do something, usually of a sexual nature. For many, sextortion is brutal as not only are victims forced to provide sexual pictures or to participate in unwanted sexual activities, but also in many cases the perpetrators seem to take pleasure in the pleading of their victims to end the abuse. Although the cases provided as examples in this section involve adult perpetrators, those abusers in sextortion cases include both online predators and minor's peers.

In general sextortion occurs in one of two scenarios. The first is after the end of an intimate or sexual relationship during which sexual pictures or images were taken of one or both partners. The second is after an online encounter in which the victim provides the perpetrator a sexual image either taken by the victim themselves or another. For teens, both scenarios are likely.[22]

In these scenarios, perpetrators are likely to contact their victims via the online community. Some perpetrators utilize social networking sites such as Facebook or Instagram and some perpetrators utilize dating apps such as Tinder or Bumble. Perpetrators are also known to use messaging platforms such as Snapchat, Skype, and email. The majority of the initial images were voluntarily provided to the perpetrator by the victim. However, in some cases, perpetrators acquire images via software loaded on the victim's computer which triggers web cameras without the knowledge of the victim or other recorded images made through hidden cameras without the victim's consent.

Unfortunately, once the initial images are the property of the perpetrators, demands for more sexually explicit images are made. The teens perceive that their only option to avoid humiliation is to comply with the demands of their abuser. For many teens, those required more sexually explicit images include sexual acts such as masturbation, sexual activities with animals or inanimate objects, sexual activity with another, or more images of genitalia or other nudity. In addition, for some teens the demands through sextortion include face-to-face meetings for the purpose of sexual activity either with their offender or with another person of their offender's choosing.

For many child victims, it is difficult to understand the concept of sextortion as many have never considered the impact of blackmail. They may have been forced by a sibling to unload the dishwasher or feed the dog in exchange for a sibling's silence on a bad grade in school or a dent in the family car; however, they have no concept of blackmail and its long-term consequences. With sextortion, the threat of revealing pornographic images or their videoed sexual actions (with another person or an object such as a hairbrush) is devastating to the child, as would be the outcomes for adults involved in the same situation. However, as adults may be concerned about their reputations if these images or videos were released, a child is concerned about the reputation among peers and the reactions of their parents to their sexuality and the legal community for producing and distributing child pornography.

Essentially, teen victims will comply with the demands of their perpetrators to avoid the embarrassment associated with the perpetrator's threats.[23] Those threats include posting images online, sending the images to their parents or friends, and sending the images to law enforcement. Therefore, many teens have the potential of being a victim of sextortion. In most cases, the fear of parental knowledge or the fear of disappointing their parents is the most common reasons for teens allowing the sextortion to continue.

HOW DO I PROTECT MY CHILD?

As a parent, we often ignore the impact we have upon the action of our children. With sexting, the action is almost considered a norm in teen society; hence, telling our teenagers to not participate in sexting seems to be a waste of time and language. However, in some instances, based upon the relationships between teens and parents, conversations about the negative consequences of sexting may be enough to prevent the child from participating in sexting. These will not be first-time conversations but rather conversations that are based upon over-the-years conversations on safety, teen life, and peer relationships. For parents, who have not had a pattern of "keeping you safe" conversations with their children, a first-time conversation on sexting will most likely be difficult and awkward for both parties.

In cases where parents and teens do not easily converse on the subject of sexuality, sexting may not be the best focus of the conversation. For these individuals, the concept of privacy and the right to privacy by their child may be a more appealing topic as related to sexting. Regardless, parents should be aware of the conditions that exist within their teen's life prior to their involvement in sexting and recognize those conditions as rational for their teen's use of sext messages.

Although parents were all teens at one time, technology was not a critical part of their lives. For teens today, it is more unusual for them not to have a cell phone and text than for them to have a cell phone and text. Hence, parents must realize what today's children and teens experience and be willing to participate in cell phone spot-checks if they are concerned about the activities of their children. These attempts, just as with other discussions on proactive approaches to address ICAC, include open and continued lines of communication between the child and parent as well as parental supervision.

In addition, parents who are themselves experienced online will have children who are experienced online. Parents who are not experienced online will also have children who are experienced online. Therefore, the higher levels of online literacy by our teens reduce the likelihood that online parental controls will limit their activities. In addition, as children age, parents are less likely to monitor their online activities. Parents and teens must continually communicate throughout their children's lifetime for their safety against ICAC.

Finally, parents must acknowledge that although they are proactive in protecting their children from ICAC, not all parents are proactive.[24] Hence, parents should warn their children against distributing sexual language or sexual images to others. In addition, parents should warn their children against distributing text or images that generally report or document any form of illegal activity. Also, it should be noted that, for those teens without parental supervision, their vulnerabilities may increase the vulnerability in the teens with proactive parents. Since sexting is an action among peers, it will include not only your teen but also those teens at risk for victimization.

Therefore, parents must communicate to their children their own willingness to help them if the children ever feel as though they are a victim of their own self-initiated sexting. By providing teens this notion of acceptance and forgiveness, parents will be better able to protect their children from the dangers of sexting and the most negative outcome of sextortion.

SUMMARY

Cyberspace and cell phone technology allow teens and preteens to communicate with others throughout the world and without the permission of their parents. However, in many cases, parents are surprised to learn that their children are communicating with individuals that they would perceive as inappropriate.

In 2000 when Congress enacted the CIPA as an attempt to limit a child's exposure to obscene or harmful content received via the Internet, it is doubtful that Congress considered that children could themselves be responsible for the initial contact with their abuser. However, time has shown that, in many cases of ICAC, to include cases facilitated through sexting, the teen or preteen were often the ones initiating contact with individuals who will expose them to those obscene materials.

As parents, we ignore the impact we have upon our children. In some instances, based upon the relationships between teens and parents, conversations about the negative consequences of sexting may be enough to prevent the child from participating in sexting. In others, monitoring the teens' activities on the cell phone provided to them by the parents is necessary.

Parents must be aware that in today's world of technology and cell phone availability, teens are now more at risk of victimization from their own initiated interactions with online abusers. Two of these more common forms of victimization are sexting and the most negative outcome of sextortion. Thus, for parents, the question of whether their child or teen is the victim or perpetrator of sexting is often answered with—yes, to at least one or both.

To reduce their child's likelihood of victimization, parents must be willing and able to discuss sexuality and sexting with their children to help avoid these types of ICAC. Through open and consistent communications as well as rules on cell phone usage, parents may help to prevent their children being a victim of sexting or sextortion.

Chapter Five

Cyberbullying

Brianna is an outgoing sixteen-year-old blonde with a new boyfriend named Chase. Lately, her mother Susan has been noticing that Brianna appears anxious when receiving text messages via her cell phone. Upon receiving her most recently observed text, Susan asks Brianna if her boyfriend is texting her. Brianna replies that, no, but that his ex-girlfriend is sending her messages warning Brianna to stay away from Chase. Brianna shows Susan the text messages, which not only are meant to frighten Brianna but also threaten to destroy her reputation and her car, and to hurt her friends.

Historically, parents of teens and preteens have worried about their children's safety when out in public, when driving with peers, and when their children attended parties and social events with other teens. For these parents, the concerns were of underage drinking, unprotected sex, and other risky activities which may cause physical harm or even an accidental death to their child. Today, those concerns still exist; however, in the world of technology and cyberspace, those parental worries have been expanded to include bullying, intimidation, and victimization via the online community.[1] Specifically, for today's parents, the worry that their teen (or preteen) will be a victim of bullying or cyberbullying is very real and for parents who have had children or know of children who have been victims of cyberbullying, this type of abuse is one of their most current fears for their children. In cyberspace, cyberbullying is an action deserving of parental attention.[2]

Cyberbullying, an extension of bullying, is defined as the use of technology (usually by a teen or preteen) to include a cell phone, a computer, instant messaging, or social networking sites to harass, threaten, or intimidate another.[3] In these cases, another is a teen or preteen—therefore someone's child or children. Hence, this chapter is designed to serve as a guide for parents attempting to reduce the risk of their child becoming a victim of cyberbullying or participating in the cyberbullying of another. This chapter provides information to parents on cyberbullying statistics and summaries of famous cases of cyber-bullying. In addition, this chapter attempts to provide explanations as to why some children are victims of cyberbullying while others are not, provides parents a working knowledge of laws enacted to address bullying or cyberbullying in the United States, and to provide sugges-tions for parents (and school administrators) who are actively attempt-ing to protect their children from becoming victims or perpetrators of cyberbullying. However, prior to specific discussions on the topic of cyberbullying, parents must first understand the action of bullying and the dynamics behind bullying as well as how to recognize the vulner-abilities and subtle signs of victimization often demonstrated by their children who are being victimized.

ELEMENTS OF BULLYING

The term bullying has been used to cover a wide range of behaviors toward others to include hazing, teasing, physical attacks, and sexual assaults.[4] Few parents have entered and exited childhood without either being a victim of bullying or a perpetrator of bullying. However, these actions should not be considered normal. In this discussion, bullying is defined in terms of general actions that involve the intent to cause fear or harm to the victim. Although bullying often peaks during the middle school years, cyberbullying may extend throughout high school.[5]

Bullies do not randomly select their victims.[6] Common traits of bul-lies include the desire for control, an ability to manipulate others, and the perception that their victims are inferior. Hence, bullies perceive their victims, because of some level of weakness or vulnerability, deserve the action of bullying.

In examining the family structure of bullies, in most cases, the action is a result of a learned behavior.[7] Bullies are often exposed to violence and intimidation in their own homes. They then continue these behaviors, with themselves as the bully, outside of their home. Unfortunately for parents, knowledge of the violence within a bully's home and an explanation for the dynamics behind the bully's actions does little to reduce the victimization of their children by that bully.

Bullying is not unique in the teen arena. In all cases of bullying, several elements exist which facilitate the outcome of someone being bullied. Those elements include: (1) an imbalance of or inequality in power; (2) a threat of harm; and, (3) the result of fear or terror.[8]

Historically, in cases of bullying, the imbalance of power is an imbalance of physical strength and stature. In other words, the larger or older child bullied the smaller or younger child. Today, we also see that notion of an imbalance of power or inequality when one teen is successful while another teen is not successful. For example, in cheerleading, if two individuals try out for the same position but only one is successful, the result may be teasing or threats (i.e., bullying) by the unsuccessful teen toward the successful teen, or vice versa—the successful teen feels better than the unsuccessful teen, therefore bullies the other.

The threat that is expressed through bullying is usually a threat of physical harm from the larger "bully" to the smaller "victim." In these cases, "larger" does not always indicate physical size but could also indicate a higher social standing in the world of teenagers. These groups of individuals or cliques of teens are often involved in bullying. For clarity, a teen clique is a group of teenagers who place themselves together to establish some sort of familiarity or common connection. Cliques are the primary networks in which adolescents socialize. Cliques are also the structures through which teens often tease, taunt, and bully other nonclique members. Through the actions of cliques, your child may be humiliated, embarrassed, or even attacked.

Finally, fear or terror is the outcome produced from bullying.[9] Historically the victim feared or was terrorized by the knowledge that they would be subjected to physical pain, harm, and embarrassment at the hands of their bully. These fears have not been diminished within the teen world. These three common elements of bullying allow the bully or bullies to maintain power and control over victims and often coerce actions or behaviors from these victims for their benefit. The elements of cyberbullying, although theoretically similar to the elements of bullying may include name-calling, embarrassment, physical pain, and harm;[10] however, cyberbullying is not limited to immediate consequences such as physical harm and often includes emotional torture, public humiliation, and other long-term negative consequences.[11]

BULLYING TO CYBERBULLYING

For all the negative outcomes of bullying, the most positive consequence is that it is real world, personal, and immediate. This is a strange statement to read; however, in traditional cases of bullying, the victim knows the source of the bullying and knows, for the most part, why they are a victim of bullying. In other words, the victim is being bullied because they are blamed for a relationship break-up, they were recognized for an accomplishment while their bully was not, or they have more material possessions than their bully. Thus, in historical cases of bullying, the victim knows their bully or bullies and is in the physical proximity of their bully during their victimization. Unfortunately, with cyberbullying this is not always true as the victim may not know who or why or when the bullying may occur.

Cyberbullying exists within the boundless cyberspace. Hence, individuals (adults and children) with the technology skills and the ability to hide behind pseudonymous names can disguise their true identities from their victims from their online community. This secrecy provides the bullies the ability to increase their aggression without identifying themselves; thus, the luxury of an attack without the probability of detection. In addition, victims of cyberbullying may be misled about the identity of their bully to the point that (in the victim's mind) their bully is a significant member in their social arena with many supporters when, in actuality, their bully is only a minor character in the reality of their lives and has little or no influence over others.[12]

The power for many bullies in the action of cyberbullying is related to their anonymity and the false identity that they impress upon their victim.[13] It is this anonymous power of the cyberbully that parents must acknowledge as being perceived as significant to their children in order that the parents help reduce their children's likelihood of emotional trauma through being a victim of cyberbullying.

CYBERBULLYING AND SUICIDE

The National Crime Victimization Survey suggests that nearly 30 percent of students ages twelve to eighteen are victims of bullying at school on an annual basis.[14] The Urban Institute suggests that nearly 20 percent of students are victims of cyberbullying on an annual basis and that females are nearly twice as likely as males to be victims of cyberbullying.[15] In addition, a most severe outcome of bullying and cyberbullying is fatal. The following describes five of the more significant cases of cyberbullying—all of which resulted in the suicide of the teen victim. These cases are presented to you, the parent, to provide an awareness of the cases and information and details which you may utilize as examples and actual events in talking to your children about victimization through cyberbullying.

Ryan Halligan (1989–2003)

In October 2003, Ryan Halligan died of suicide by hanging.[16] Ryan, a thirteen-year-old victim of bullying and cyberbullying, made the decision to end his pain after an online rejection and humiliation by a girl in his class.

Ryan's life was not unique to a preteen male. Throughout Ryan's life, things were difficult for him. Although Ryan's family was loving and supportive, he struggled with school and social or peer relationships. Upon entering kindergarten, Ryan was placed in special education classes to help address some of his developmental challenges at the academic level. His social interactions among peers within his age cohort were limited and, for several years, his most frequent social interactions were with teachers and family members.

In the fifth grade, it was known that Ryan was bullied and beaten at least on one occasion by a male classmate. He also experienced teasing and taunting by his classmates for not being athletic and physically weak. During Ryan's sixth and seventh grade years, he continued to struggle with his schoolwork and social interactions. The bullying increased as rumors of homosexuality surfaced. When Ryan's eighth grade year started, he began an online social interaction with a girl in his class. Unfortunately, while Ryan shared his most intimate feelings with the girl, she shared these conversations with her friends to embarrass him. When the girl rejected him through repeated IMs, which she posted on websites, blogs, and other forms of social media, Ryan's rejection in their "relationship" was public. That humiliation of rejection then exposed to the online community was the final act of cyberbullying against Ryan, who ended his own life. Although no criminal charges were filed, within a year of Ryan's suicide, Vermont legislators signed their Bullying Prevention Law.

Megan Meier (1992–2006)

In October 2006, Megan Taylor Meier died of suicide by hanging.[17.] Megan, a thirteen-year-old victim of cyberbullying, made the decision to end her pain after being rejected by a person posing as a sixteen-year-old boy.

Megan Meier had been under the care of a psychiatrist since she had expressed to her mother the desire to kill herself in the third grade. Megan struggled with depression, attention deficit disorder, and self-esteem issues. Upon opening a MySpace account in eighth grade, Megan began an online relationship with a person she thought was a sixteen-year-old boy named Josh who was homeschooled. Weeks into the relationship, "Josh" rejected Megan and began posting cruel messages to an online bulletin about Megan and her treatment toward some of her peers. Through AOL's Instant Messenger, the last few exchanges between the couple occurred. Minutes after the last exchange, Megan hung herself in her bedroom closet.

Later it was discovered that Josh never existed. In fact, weeks later it was uncovered that "Josh" was the mother of a neighborhood girl who, at one time, had been a friend of Megan's and who claimed to be upset over Megan's treatment toward her daughter. As there were no formal laws prohibiting cyberbullying, in 2008 Missouri legislators approved a bill to include penalties for bullying via computer or other electronic devices within their state laws.

Jessica Logan (1990–2008)

In July 2008, Jessica Logan died of suicide by hanging.[18] Jessica, a victim of cyberbullying as the result of a nude Spring Break picture of herself, made the decision to end her life after returning from the funeral for a friend.

Jessica Logan was an eighteen-year-old Ohio girl who had sent a nude image of herself (sexting) to her boyfriend. When they broke up, the boyfriend sent the picture to other girls within their high school. These girls then began posting the image on a variety of social media sites including MySpace and Facebook to embarrass and ridicule Jessica—it worked.

After returning from a funeral for a friend who had also committed suicide and, feeling as though the cyberbullying would continue forever, Jessica made the decision to end her life. Not only is this a case of cyberbullying, it is also a case of victimization via sexting. In 2012, Ohio's governor signed the Jessica Logan Act, which expanded the state's anti-bullying law to prohibit harassment by electronic means—in other words, to prohibit cyberbullying.

Hope Witsell (1996–2009)

In September 2009, Hope Witsell died of suicide by hanging.[19] Hope, a thirteen-year-old victim of cyberbullying and sexting, made the decision to end her life after returning to school in the fall and realizing that the cyberbullying that had started at the end of the last school year from sexting was continuing.

Hope Witsell was a thirteen-year-old girl in Florida with a boyfriend. In the spring of 2009, Hope sent a topless picture of herself to her boyfriend. Another student, after seeing the picture on the boy's cell phone, distributed the picture to other students within the surrounding schools. The name-calling, obscenities, and cyberbullying began and continued throughout the remainder of the school year. Through MySpace and Facebook, the cyberbullying was facilitated and, upon returning to school in September, Hope realized that the bullying and cyberbullying had not ended. In reaction, Hope wrote a suicide note and hung herself. Not only was this a tragic case of cyberbullying, it also demonstrates the potentially destructive outcomes of sexting in young people's lives.

Tyler Clementi (1991–2010)

In September 2010, a quiet but kind Tyler Clementi jumped to his death from the George Washington Bridge.[20] Tyler, an eighteen-year-old freshman in college, made the decision to end his life after a video capturing Tyler and another male kissing was released on the Internet.

Tyler Clementi, described as a nice young man from a supportive family, had experienced some verbal bullying earlier in his life as he was not the athlete that many expected in high school males. Tyler was quiet and often reserved in his social actions with peers. Later, after graduating from high school and enrolling at Rutgers, Tyler's roommate placed a hidden webcam in their dorm room and recorded an encounter with Tyler and another male. The roommate then posted the sexual encounter on Twitter. Tyler was embarrassed and humiliated within his dorm community and the online community. Just three days after the encounter, Tyler jumped to his death leaving behind a suicide note. Not only was the case of Tyler Clementi a case of cyberbullying, it also began a focus on the awareness of LGBT teens and cyberbullying through New Jersey's 2010 Anti-Bullying Bill of Rights.

COMMON CASE ELEMENTS

When reviewing the elements of the provided cases of cyberbullying which resulted in the teens' suicides, many similarities exist within the lives of the victims. In addition, many preconceptions of the "typical" victim of cyberbullying are not shown to exist. In historical cases of bullying, one presumes that the bully is older or physically larger in statue, egocentric, or from a higher socioeconomic stratum than the victim. However, those characteristics of bullies are not as common in cases of cyberbullying. Specifically, none of the five cases discussed in this chapter involved a bully significantly older or physically larger than the victim. In addition, in none of the cases discussed was it determined that the cyberbully was from a higher socioeconomic stratum than the victim and, in none of the cases, did it appear as though the cyberbully was egocentric. In fact, the use of the Internet and social media as the mode of bullying suggest that the cyberbully was not overly confident or aggressive as these cases were not confrontational or on a face-to-face basis but rather hidden under the cover of the virtual world. Thus, the cyberbullies in these cases were not easily identified nor classified.

In terms of similarities in these cases, many existed. In considering the age of the victims, all were not the same age, but the victims were at a crossroads in terms of their age and life-stage development. Specifically, three of the victims were thirteen years old—the time of transition from middle school to high school. As some teens suggest, this is the time when you begin to realize who you are and who you are not. Specifically, the teens who perhaps participated in sports at the local or regional recreational level, where everyone must play, begin to realize that in their school's sports teams, not everyone will be selected or even play. In another example of the life change from middle to high school, the teen who throughout their years of education has been at the top of the class in performance and grades may not continue in that academic position once enrolled in courses with other "top students" from surrounding schools. The teen whose identity has been the "smart one" may no longer be the smartest in their classes.

Finally, as all parents know, at age thirteen, teens are beginning to develop physically, however, not all at the same rate or time. If a child, especially a girl, begins to develop at a faster rate than her peers, then the notion of her sexuality or sexual activity may begin to emerge among her classmates. Along the same lines, if a teen, particularly a boy, is slower than his peers in beginning to develop physically, then the questions about his sexuality or manliness may begin to emerge among his classmates. Being physically different from your peers is sometimes one of the reasons for the bullying or cyberbullying but not the only reason.

Within the cases discussed, two of the teen victims were eighteen; hence, dismissing the myth that victims of cyberbullying are only the younger teens. The age of eighteen, also another critical age in the development of a young person, is the time in which that young person begins to decide their place in the world. During this time, young people are usually out of high school and are either working at a job or in college. They often perceive the world as watching for their next step—are they going to be perceived as successful or a failure? The pressures that parents experienced when they were eighteen are increased for young people today. For parents, if they made a poor decision at eighteen, then usually only their family and close friends knew of that mistake and few discussed the events. For today's eighteen-year-olds, if they make a poor decision, then, through social media, everyone knows and many conversations occur on the topic of the mistake.

Three of the five victims were female. This is not to suggest that females are the more likely victims of cyberbullying although, officially, females are more likely to report being a victim of cyberbullying. However, current research on cyberbullying suggests that not only is gender related to the likelihood of victimization via cyberbullying, but also that gender (being female) is related to the propensity to perpetrate instances of cyberbullying. The notion of *Mean Girls* does exist in the world of cyberbullying.[21]

In terms of victimization, historically it was not unusual for male victims of cyberbullying to also be victims of physical bullying. Currently, it is becoming more common for female victims of cyberbullying to also have been a victim of physical bullying. In male victims, the explanation is common sense and traditional bullying—they are often smaller, more feminine in their actions, or perceived as physically weaker than their perpetrators. The cyberbullying of the victim is often based around a common theme of homosexuality or the inability to navigate the social or peer interactions common in middle or high school.[22] This is the male student who talks excessively about subjects that are not of interest to most of the members of his age cohort (e.g., the magnitude of flight for the latest Phantom 4 Drone) or the young male who is unable to understand the subtle actions that indicate a lack of interest (e.g., a person who does not know if they are available for an outing for four consecutive Saturdays is not interested in spending time with them). However, the male perpetrators of cyberbullying, unlike the male perpetrators of traditional bullying, are of the same physical size as their victims and utilize the online community as the means by which they ridicule or humiliate their victims in an attempt to gain online recognition or notoriety, which would be significant in their virtual world.

Females involved in cyberbullying may or may not exist in what one would consider a traditional bullying environment. Females who participate in the bullying of other females usually do so to maintain their higher social standing in their school's social network.[23] At the heart of the bullying incidents involving females is a conflict within a dating relationship. The bullying begins when a male chooses one female over the other; hence, the female begins bullying that chosen female. This is the same situation which occurs in same-sex relationships as the rejected party will often attempt to bully the romantically desired party.

In cases of cyberbullying, a rejection of a relationship (either direct or indirect) may also be at the heart of the matter.[24] However, cyberbullying may be more of a result of indirect rejection, the perpetrators were never rejected from their person of interest (POI) as they were never involved in a physical (in the same room) relationship with that person.

Unfortunately, from the perpetrator's perspective, they were in a relationship with their POI and now that relationship has been jeopardized. The victim of cyberbullying is perceived as a threat to the cyberbully's relationship given that they are now or were in a relationship with the perpetrator's POI. An example of this would be that one female continually texts and perhaps sexts a male; however, even though the male responds, he is uninterested in a relationship with her as his interests are with another female. Hence, the first female cyberbullies the second as she perceives her as a threat to her "relationship." In cases of cyberbullying, as discussed, the virtual world allows the individual to hide in the anonymity within the online community while they ridicule, harass, and even threaten their victim. In other words, they cyberbully without the fear of identification, blame, or retribution.

Finally, as described in the case studies, one final and fatal result of being a victim of cyberbullying is suicide.[25] Although only a small number of cyberbullying cases result in a suicide, it is a potential outcome that parents that must recognize. All victims of cyberbullying experience some form of embarrassment or public humiliation. In the cases described, most victims of cyberbullying experienced or perceived either a direct or an indirect rejection from a romantic relationship. In all cases described, the victim experienced the betrayal of the details of their most intimate thoughts or actions. Unlike victims of bullying twenty years ago, a rejection or humiliation from a relationship would be known to a small group of friends and family.[26] In today's world of cyberbullying, a rejection or humiliation from another party is known to everyone who has access to the online community. For teen victims who spend much of their lives within the online community texting and messaging their connections, links, or "friends," humiliation within the environment, which is most significant in their lives, are simply too much for these individuals to ignore.

WHY ARE CERTAIN CHILDREN TARGETS?

As parents, we always want to know how we can protect our children—protecting them from cyberbullying is no different. Theories of victimization rarely suggest that victims are randomly selected. In fact, most theories suggest either an active or passive role of participation by the victim prior to their victimization. In cases of bullying and cyberbullying, the role of the victim is that of passive participation. By identifying the factors that exist in many cases of cyberbullying within cyberspace, we are better able to explain why some children are targeted while others are not targeted. In the overwhelming majority of cyberbullying cases those characteristics of victims are either demographic or behavioral.[27] As some teens suggest, the person was a victim of cyberbullying because they were perceived by the peers as "annoying."

As with traditional cases of bullying, victims are in many cases smaller in physical stature or perceived as physically weaker than their peers. In other cases, victims of bullying and cyberbullying are overweight, have a strong body odor, or attempt to dress to a role not in their identity (e.g., dress as a jock when they do not play sports or dress as a "gangster" when they are very shy and reserved). In other cases of bullying and cyberbullying, victims exhibit antisocial behaviors, act like "little professors" or socialize with very few friends. In addition, many victims of bullying have low levels of self-esteem and are insecure and anxious. During the teenage years, these characteristics are more common. Finally, in traditional cases of bullying, it is not unusual for victims to have been identified as developmentally (intellectually or physically) delayed.[28] Whereas many of the characteristics of victims of bullying also apply to cyberbullying, rarely are the victims of cyberbullying physically disabled. However, it is not unusual for victims of cyberbullying to suffer from low self-esteem, have academic challenges, and possess other mental disabilities such as the inability to be flexible on actions, procedures, and rules of play (e.g., no "do-overs").

In terms of parental presence in the lives of teen victims of bullying, the characteristics are common. In fact, in many cases of traditional bullying and cyberbullying, it is the perception by their bullies that the parents assume responsibilities for the child. The parent chooses their child's clothes, their child's afterschool activities, and their child's hobbies. Specifically, often, male victims of bullying and cyberbullying, because of their perceived relationship with their parents (particularly their mother) are called a "mama's boy," a "titty baby," or a "hot mama" as a result of the peer perceptions of an overprotective parent. For female victims of cyberbullying, the perception of being a princess or easy (i.e., slut) by their peers opens the door for bullying and cyberbullying.

Victims of bullying and cyberbullying also may passively demonstrate their willingness to allow bullying to occur. In cases such as these, perpetrators of bullying often observe their victims failing to prohibit the bullying of others. From the perpetrator's perspective, their victims are not likely to report the bullying of others; hence, probably not likely to report the victimization of themselves. From a perpetrator's perspective, if the victim of bullying or cyberbullying is not willing to defend themselves, then they allow the abuse to continue.

Finally, it is not unusual for victims of bullying to attempt to befriend their bully.[29] From the victim's perspective, if they are "friends" with the bully, they are less likely to be the continued victim of the bully. In addition, it is not unusual for victims of bullying to begin to participate in the bullying or cyberbullying of others.

Haley (age 16) transferred to a new high school at the end of her 9th grade year. At the end of the year, she was considered well liked and popular. In fact, she tried out for cheerleading, made the cheerleading squad, and began dating one of the more popular football players. Unfortunately, the football player was previously involved in a relationship with another cheerleader. For months, until Haley and the young man stopped seeing each other, she was a victim of cyberbullying via text messages posted to social media sites.

In terms of cyberbullying, parents should understand that the targets of victims are usually wider than the targets for traditional bullying given that the potential for perpetrators is wider. Essentially, cyberbullying provides the opportunity to bully an individual without the face-to-face confrontation in traditional cases of bullying.[30] In addition, a cyberbully may choose to target a victim not because of a perceived wrong to them but because of a perceived wrong to another with the protection of the anonymity of the online community to facilitate the abuse.

LEGAL EFFORTS TO REDUCE CYBERBULLYING

In extreme cases, bullying and cyberbullying may be addressed under laws prohibiting discriminatory harassment if based upon race, color, sex, age, religion or disability.[31] In addition, civil rights laws that could be violated in extreme cases of cyberbullying are Titles IV and Title VI of the Civil Rights Act of 1964, Title IX of the 1972 Education Amendments, and Title II and Title III of the 1990 Americans with Disabilities Act. Therefore, laws related to bullying and cyberbullying have been initiated within various states across the country.

As of January 2016, all fifty states as well as the District of Columbia have enacted laws to prevent bullying. An example of these efforts is Montana's Bully-Free Montana Act (H. Be. 0284) signed by their governor in 2015 which prohibits harassment via electronic means if the action is "with the purpose to terrify, intimidate, threaten, harass, annoy, or offend . . . with a person by electronic communications and uses obscene, lewd, or profane language, suggests a lewd or lascivious act, or threatens to inflict injury or physical harm to the person or property of the person." In addition, the overwhelming majority of the states include the phrase "electronic harassment" in their legislative language and nearly half of the states define or include the term "cyberbullying" in their law. An example of this use of a definition in a state law includes Nevada's S.B. 163 (chapter 188) which specifically states that "Cyber-bullying means bullying through the use of electronic communications." Although considered trivial to many, the definition of cyberbullying is critical in addressing victimization. And this use of the term cyberbullying is significant in prevention. In many ways, similar to legislation in the 1980s related to computer hacking, until the phrase was defined, it was unclear as to what action was being prohibited.

Given that the victims and perpetrators in cases of cyberbullying are within the setting of the school environment, the majority of state cyberbullying laws require a school policy to prevent cyberbullying. An example of this effort includes California's A.B. 9 "Seth's Law" (2011) which requires school policies and investigation into possible cases of bullying and cyberbullying after Seth Walsh (age thirteen) committed suicide after being harassed about his sexual orientation. Some states such as North Carolina have extended school policies to prohibit the cyberbullying of a school employee by a student (§14-458.2); and New Jersey has extended school policies to include incidents that take place "off school grounds [but] that substantially disrupts or interferes with the orderly operations of the school" (P.L. 2010, chapter 122).

Finally, in terms of penalties, states support school-sanctioned punishments for bullying and cyberbullying. In addition (as of January 2016), eighteen states impose criminal sanctions for those found guilty of bullying or cyberbullying. Those states are: Alaska, Arkansas, Colorado, Idaho, Iowa, Kentucky, Louisiana, Maryland, Mississippi, Missouri, Montana, Nevada, New Jersey, North Carolina, North Dakota, Tennessee, Washington, and Wisconsin. From a parent's perspective, if your state does not have specific laws pertaining to cyberbullying, it may be embedded in antiharassment legislation or it may be time for you as a parent to place a call to your elected officials.[32]

HOW CAN I PROTECT MY CHILD?

To protect your child, all aspects of victimization must be recognized. Attempts to explain the risk of victimization in the 1970s examined predatory crimes in terms of three elements: (1) a likely target; (2) a motivated offender; and (3) the absence of capable guardians.[33] In cases of predatory crime, we must recognize that there will always exist a target (or individual) with the potential for victimization. In addition, we must also consider that there will always be an offender or individual with the motivation (whether it be financial or ego) to prey upon another. Finally, we must acknowledge that without the ability to prohibit the victimization or a guardian of the target, the victimization is likely to occur. Again, in attempting to protect your child or children from the victimization that results from cyberbullying, a parent must recognize and address all elements of a predatory crime.[34]

In considering the target for victimization via cyberbullying or your child, a parent should first consider the general characteristics of victims of bullying. Again, in cases of bullying or cyberbullying, victims are usually perceived as either easy prey or competition to the offender. So how do we help our children to not be perceived as "easy prey"? The first step is by honestly examining the physical and behavioral characteristics of your children. This is not to suggest that children who are physically smaller should be provided growth hormones or that children with shy personalities should be enrolled in self-defense classes, but simply that parents must acknowledge the strengths and weaknesses in their children as these characteristics may place them at risk or protect them from victimization via cyberbullying. This is not an easy task for parents and it is suggested that these characteristics of their children may be better recognized from someone else in the family or close social circle.

Ask yourself these questions. Is your child physically small? Is your child an introvert? Does your child have only a few friends? For the most part, if children's behavior is not considered unusual within their age cohort, even those of a smaller or slower developing physical build, then they are not a likely victim of cyberbullying. In fact, for the most part, it is the behaviors of the children or teens that places them in the position of victimization. Young people who are victims of cyberbullying have in some way (passive or active) offended their bully. This offense may have been through a passive action such as continuing to speak or answer the teacher when questions are posed to the class or an active action such as replacing an object of affection (e.g., being the new girlfriend).

For parents attempting to reduce the likelihood of cyberbullying for their children, measures should be taken during the developmental stages of the children's growth to not only reduce victimization but to also increase the socialization skills of their children; thus, helping to protect your children from being perceived as "different" from their peers. In today's era of text messages, voice mail, and email, basic one-on-one communication skills are lost. Today's parents must work harder to help their children protect themselves.

One of the best things a parent can do for their child is to introduce them (at an early age) to children their own age. Parents will state that their children communicate much better with adults than individuals their own age, and that is a great accomplishment; however, as children continue to develop they will be placed in social situations involving peers their own age (e.g., school, sports, music classes) and the development of communication skills within that group is critical in the prevention of bullying or cyberbullying. By involving your child, at an early age, in same-age activities within your community, you are reducing your child's risk of being considered an outsider and targeted for bullying. Also important during this strategy of child involvement, and for many parents the more difficult aspect, is not immersing themselves into the child's activities. As parents we want to help our child be successful. We want to be the parent who attends all the class field trips, the parent who drives the carpools, and the parents who brings the Friday classroom snacks every week; however, does this really help our children to become independent? For many parents, this help is sometimes allowing the child to venture on their own, even if it means we watch their social interactions from across a playground or only for a few minutes of the activity (e.g., the first ten minutes and last fifteen minutes of a two-hour practice). Again, this strategy to allow for the social interactions of your child among peers begins early and continues throughout the teen years of development and is sometimes the most difficult help that a parent can provide.

In considering the offender in cases of cyberbullying, most are motivated by an original action either passive or active by the young victim. Unfortunately, just as with models of crime prevention, one must acknowledge that there will always exist individuals or bullies in search of victims.[35] From this aspect, parents' most critical role is in attempting to reduce the likelihood that their children will become a bully. This is addressed from two avenues—the first in that your child is the bully, primary or secondary, and the second in that your child either facilitates the bullying of another or is a bystander to the bullying of another.

For parents concerned that their children may be the bully or a part of a bullying network that victimizes others, addressing this situation is critical. Children, in many cases, model the behaviors of their parents. Parents who are in an aggressive job position may not see the alpha male (or female) behaviors in their children. In many cases, these are the parents who receive calls from school officials to discuss aggressive or violent behaviors by the child toward another while in school. For those parents, who may become irritated or upset by a call from an administrator, consider the call or contact as a sign of potential future problems unless these behaviors are addressed immediately and directly. Unfortunately, most parents are not concerned about their children as the bully, which leaves more of a burden on the parent of the child victim. For parents of the children who participate in the bullying or cyberbullying of another, as with any inappropriate or undesirable behavior, consequences and sanctions exist to address those behaviors. The bullying or cyberbullying of a child by your children should also have consequences.

For the parents concerned that their children are facilitating the bullying or cyberbullying of another child by either identifying young people for others to victimize of by not acting in the defense of a bullying victim, it must be acknowledged that these behaviors (although not desirable) are often the behaviors seen in the adult world. In the workplace, it is not unusual for employees to sacrifice each other or steal each other's ideas to better or to protect themselves. It is also not unusual for employees to witness firsthand the mistreatment of others and to allow the behaviors to continue. Therefore, how do we as parents teach our children to stand up for others when we often fail to do so ourselves? Again, the notion of modeling behavior is important and communication is significant. As parents, we can usually recall a situation from our childhood where we witnessed another child or teen being mistreated by a peer or group of peers. For some of us, we stood up and defended the individual being mistreated; for most of us, we did nothing. Even though we failed to act, we all still remember the scenario—as a parent, this can still be a "teachable moment," a "do as I say not as I did" example. By parents discussing the situation that they witnessed as a young person (and perhaps the guilt they felt for not intervening) an example of why you should not allow victimization to occur is illustrated to your child.

Finally, in considering the notion of guardians or the absence of capable guardians,[36] parents should introduce the notion that a guardian is not simply a teacher or school official. In fact, many potential cases of victimization are eliminated when offenders feel as though they are being observed; hence, these offenders will not act for fear of being identified. In cases of bullying or cyberbullying, guardians can be teachers, school officials, and parents, but they can also be ISPs that screen for specific words or phrases.[37] Thus, by explaining to your child that obscenities, vulgar language, or lewd suggestions are not appropriate and sometimes punishable through computer crime legislation, parents may, in fact, provide guardians against their children's victimization without the physical presence of a person.

Unfortunately, even with the best of preventive measures, some children will be victims of cyberbullying. As parents, you need to acknowledge that your child may be that victim. If you feel as though your child is a victim of bullying or cyberbullying, you should ask. Keep in mind that for many teens reporting victimization by peers to your parents is embarrassing. It acknowledges that they are not liked by their peers and that, in fact, they are disliked by their peers. For parents, the reaction to this report by the child is critical. Practice your "game face." When your child or teen reports to you being a victim of cyberbullying—listen and do not criticize or offer the quick advice of "just stand up to your bully." Keep in mind, that in cases of cyberbullying, the teens may not know the identity of their bully. In addition, if the teens suspect the identity of their cyberbully, they still may not want a confrontation. If the case exists where your teenagers do not know the identity (or identities) of their cyberbully, however, the bullying language references activities within the school environment, then you (or your teen) should contact the guidance counselor within the school to report the bullying. For the most part, schools have in place antibullying policies that apply to these situations. Through discussions with the social networks (other students) in the school the guidance counselors are often able to identify the perpetrators of cyberbullying. By identifying the perpetrator of cyberbullying, their anonymity is nonexistent; hence, the cover of the online community is greatly reduced. In addition, guidance counselors are trained in mediation and, in many cases, are able to resolve the conflict(s) between students.

If your teenager does not know the identity of their cyberbully and messages appear as though activities outside of the school environment are referenced, then you, as a parent should seek answers to cause within that venue (i.e., church activities are mentioned so talk with the youth leaders). In addition, as bullying is illegal in all fifty states and the District of Columbia, local law enforcement should be contacted. This is essential in cases of repeated, prolonged bullying in that documentation of the events will need to be provided for not only prosecution (if deemed necessary) but also protective orders (if deemed necessary).

TALKING TO YOUR CHILD

As parents, you should continue open dialogues with your children to ensure that their worries and fears on this violation are being discussed and addressed. In all five of the cases discussed in this chapter, the victims of cyberbullying felt they had no option other than suicide to end their abuse. For parents of children being bullied or cyberbullied, the natural instinct is to fix the situation for their children. However, by involving others (such as the bully's parent) you may, in fact, worsen the situation. First, talk to your children about what is happening to them. If the bullying is from an anonymous online source, a remedy may be in your children discontinuing site visits, changing password, or refraining from all online social networks for a period. As your children, do what they want you to do. If they want you to contact the school officials, then of course, you will do so; however, if they ask you not to contact school officials, please consider their request. In some instances, this will be the first opportunity for your children to solve their own problem.

For parents, allowing their children to make a mistake or to attempt to address a situation on their own is one of the most difficult parts of parenting. If the bullying or cyberbullying continues, even after your children have attempted to end the abuse, then school officials and perhaps even law enforcement should be contacted. Cyberbullying has been known to not only have devastating immediate effects on the victim, but it is also related to the long-term negative consequences of low self-esteem, anxiety, and depression into adulthood.

SUMMARY

In today's world of technology, parental worries have been expanded to include bullying, intimidation, and victimization via the online community. Specifically, for today's parents, the worry that their teen (or preteen) will be a victim of bullying or cyberbullying is a very real concern. Cyberbullying, an extension of bullying, is defined as the use of technology (usually by a teen or preteen) to include a cell phone, a computer, instant messaging, or social networking sites to harass, threaten, or intimidate another. As parents, our mission is to protect our children from harm. The effects of bullying may be long-term and extremely emotional. In addition, some long-term effects may be physical and even fatal. Bullying or cyberbullying is a real threat to today's children.

As parents, we always want to know how we can protect our children and protecting them from cyberbullying is not different. By parents rec-

t exist in many cases of cyberbullying, they are
and explain to their children why some teens and
bullying while others are not.

ing and cyberbullying may be addressed under
latory harassment if based upon race, color,
lity. In addition, civil rights laws that could be
cyberbullying include Titles IV and Title VI
964, Title IX of the 1972 Education Amend-
III of the 1990 Americans with Disabilities
es as well as the District of Columbia have
ng.

to protect their children, must recognize the signs of
and cyberbullying that are often displayed when their children
are victims. Parents must also recognize the signs that are displayed when
their children are the bullies. Through open communications and dialogues
regarding the consequences of bullying, parents can protect their children
from or assist their children in addressing bullying and cyberbullying.

Chapter Six

Cyberstalking

Lately, Hollie has been noticing that her fifteen-year-old daughter Emily has avoided leaving the house and often turns off her cell phone if she is away from home. When Hollie asks her to go to the store or run any errands, Emily provides excuses as to why she is unable to fulfill the request. Finally, Hollie asks Emily what is going on. Emily reports that she has been receiving posts to her Facebook page that report her locations and what she is doing when she is out of the house but she does not know the source of these posts.

Many individuals suggest that the constant fear of being observed, harmed, followed, embarrassed, or killed is more paralyzing than the actual act itself. These actions, as related to the victimization by another, would result in fear from a reasonable person. These actions are what sometimes are referred to as the actions associated with stalking. By definition, stalking is the obsessive and unwanted attention by an individual or groups of individuals toward another person.[1] Victims of stalking often report a fear of not knowing what will happen next, and they fear the stalking will never end. Many victims move their home, change their work or school, and even relocate their loved ones because of stalking, and other victims report missing work or school from being stalked.[2] Cyberstalking, simply stated, is online stalking or stalking in cyberspace. The goal of the cyberstalker, just as the goal for a traditional stalker, is to leave the victim feeling fearful, humiliated, and powerless.[3] Hence, cyberstalking is an ICAC that should be of concern to all parents.

According to the Bureau of Justice Statistics, over seven million people are stalked annually in the United States. Younger individuals (i.e., ages eighteen to twenty-five) experience stalking at higher rates than older individuals. In addition, over one-fourth of stalking victims are also victims of cyberstalking with younger victims even more likely to be the victims of both stalking and cyberstalking.[4] Cyberstalking is considered an ICAC and an ICAC worthy of parental attention and parental protection.[5] This chapter is intended to provide definitions, statistics, and a summary of the legislation addressing stalking and cyberstalking. Included in this chapter is information on perpetrators of stalking and cyberstalking as well as the motivation of those perpetrators. Finally, discussed in this chapter are the outcomes of stalking for the victims as well as the roles of teens in stalking and cyberstalking cases.

In the teen community, stalking is not a new concept. With the assimilation of the Internet in the daily lives of individuals, cyberstalking or the use of technology to facilitate stalking, is a very real concern for parents. Parents worry that those individuals stalking or cyberstalking their children will not only ruin the reputations and futures of their children, but that these stalkers will physically harm or even kill their children. In general, cyberstalking is an extension of the behaviors traditionally viewed as stalking; therefore, those engaged in cyberstalking are essentially stalkers.[6]

In August of 2016, Shana Grice, 19, was killed in her family home despite her previous and numerous calls to the police that she was being stalked and cyberstalked. The 27 year old man, whom she claimed was her stalker, was later arrested.[7]

Although the term "stalker" has been used since the 1500s to describe a type of prowler in criminal law, the twentieth-century definition better describes what we imagine with the act of stalking today—an individual who participates in the willful and repeated intrusions and communications with their targeted victim to the point of intimidation or producing fear.[8] Cyberstalking, the newest tool for stalking, uses technology to monitor and harass victims. Specifically, cyberstalking is an ICAC that may produce fear, harass, embarrass, and humiliate a victim. Cyberstalking is not cyber trolling (online actions that are felt to be random and spurious) as it is an action that involves a specifically targeted victim and is intentional and continuous.[9] Cyberstalking may be used financially as victims' bank accounts and credit scores may be negatively impacted, and cyberstalking may be used to harass family members, friends, and employers of victims. For parents, the cyberstalking of their children with outcomes of harassment, embarrassment, and humiliation, is a very real concern.[10]

CYBERSTALKERS AND INTERNET TROLLS

Both cyberstalkers and Internet trolls are individuals who utilize computer technology and cyberspace to commit ICAC and to monitor a victim within the online community. However, cyberstalkers usually know their victims personally and Internet trolls have rarely,[11] if ever, met their victims. The cyberstalkers' sense of power is related to the control they are able to place over their victim. The Internet troll's sense of power is related to the amount of anger and distress they can produce within the online community.[12] Hence, a cyberstalker's target is usually a single person whereas an Internet troll's target may be an individual or a group of victims.

Although their child or teen may not be the initial target of an Internet troll, parents should still be aware of their potentially negative outcomes. The Internet troll, who is usually a young male, who spends much of his time within the online community and has very few friends outside of the virtual community, desires destruction and, if their child happens to be identified by these trolls, then they may be victimized through embarrassing pictures or posts often represented as originating from the child victim or an anonymous source. For these Internet trolls, online abuse is perceived as a game and in this game, your child is the victim.

LEGAL ACTIONS TO PREVENT
STALKING AND CYBERSTALKING

In 1990, California was the first state to enact antistalking legislation.[13] This California law was in direct response to the shooting death of twenty-one-year-old actress Rebecca Schaeffer. Schaeffer, a victim of stalking for three years by Robert John Bardo, was fatally shot by her stalker in July

1989 when she opened the front door of her home. Even though Schaeffer had made repeated calls to law enforcement to report the obsessive behavior of her stalker, because her stalker was not violent and had not threatened her with violence, there was no legal recourse to intervene. Since that time, all fifty states and the District of Columbia have enacted laws against stalking; however, most stalking laws at the state level continue to require credible threats of violence toward a victim by an offender. In some cases, these threats do not occur until the stalking becomes fatal.

In 1994, the federally sponsored Violence against Women Act was signed as a part of the Violent Crime Control and Law Enforcement Act to provide funds to support the investigation and prosecution of violent crimes against women. In adult cases, the majority of the victims were, at one time, involved in a relationship with their stalker; hence, stalking was seen as a crime related to intimate partner violence. For teen victims of stalking, most are also stalked by a previous dating partner and cyberstalking is the most common mode of victimization. Unfortunately, parents often perceive stalking as an adult crime; however, social media now provides an abundance of information on victims, especially teen victims, and perpetrators are now utilizing that information to torment their victims.[14]

In 1996, President Bill Clinton signed the Interstate Stalking Act which made it illegal for someone to cross state boundaries (physically travel) with the intent to injure or harass another person, hence placing that person or the person's family in fear of injury or death. Unfortunately, as physical travel is not applicable to the online community, the act was essentially moot for cases of cyberstalking. However, in 1998, President Clinton signed the Online Child Protection Act which made it a federal crime to use any form of interstate commerce such as the telephone or the Internet to solicit or entice a child into illegal activities. Again, unfortunately, harassment for purposes other than solicitation such as stalking or cyberstalking was not included in the legislation. Thus, child and teen victims of stalking often perceive their stalking cases as never ending.

As a result, during the last decade, legislative actions have been revised and rewritten to include stalking or cyberstalking for children and adults at both the state and federal government levels. Specific examples include the 2013 Violence against Women Act, which was revised to better address the dynamics in stalking cases as well as cyberstalking which was added and defined to better address electronic communication services or systems. In 2014, the Clery Act under the 1990 Higher Education Act, which applies to crimes on college and university campuses, was amended to include stalking. Also in 2014, the 1965 Immigration and Nationality Act was revised to include stalking.

Sentences for those individuals convicted of stalking or cyberstalking may include probation, restraining orders, and prison. In those most severe cases, prison sentences vary by geographic regions and can range from eighteen months in prison to ten years and fines up to $150,000. Currently, much of US legislation designed to protect women and children also includes the prohibition of stalking.[15] In addition, most of the ICAC investigated by law enforcement entail some form of cyberstalking or harassment. For clarity, cyber harassment is similar to cyberstalking as the perpetrators usually know their victims and utilize cyberspace;[16] however, cyber harassment is actions intended to control the behavior of a victim without credible or implied threats of harm.

WHO ARE THE STALKERS AND CYBERSTALKERS?

Today there exists the debate in both public conversations and legal hearings as to what constitutes stalking. The assertion by many is that stalking is a perception on the part of the victim, and that many cases that are termed stalking are not actually cases of stalking, but rather cases of infatuation. Where one crosses the line from attraction and infatuation to stalking is often explained in terms of length of interactions and, in many cases, is clearly demonstrated. For example, a person may approach, text, or call individuals on multiple occasions for a few days, or, as with the case of California's Rebecca Schaeffer, her stalker continued his behavior for three years. Clearly the latter was a case of stalking. Unfortunately, with cyberstalking, in many cases the victims may not know if they are indeed a victim of stalking or know the identity of their stalker. These cases are especially difficult for parents and the law enforcement community as a clearly identified perpetrator of stalking or cyberstalking does not exist. Hence, to better understand stalking and cyberstalking and protect our children, parents should first consider the characteristics of stalkers.

There exist essentially five categories of stalkers. Those categories are: (1) the rejected, (2) intimacy-seeking, (3) the incompetent, (4) the resentful, and (5) the predatory.[17] The first and most common category in both adult and teen cases of stalking is the rejected stalkers. These are the individuals who usually have been in a relationship (even a very brief one) with the victim. These are the stalkers often referred to as the "crazy ex." These stalkers are angry or upset about the end of the relationship and want either the victim to return to their relationship or for the victim to be punished for the pain that they have caused them.

Parents of teens who are victims of this type of stalker should be aware that in the teen dating world, relationships are not often long-term; hence, a stalker in this category will usually not continue for long periods. In most cases, these stalkers will end their stalking once a new partner has emerged. However, for the teen that is a victim of stalking or cyberstalking, the victimization, even a brief period of victimization, may be traumatic and with long-term consequences of anxiety, stress, and fearfulness. Unfortunately, in some unique cases, this category of teen stalker, who is usually the most immediately aggressive in their actions, will be the perpetrator to utilize cyberspace, the online community, post images or defamatory statements with the sole intent to damage the reputation or humiliate their victim. It is these posts in the virtual world that continue to exist even after the stalking has ended and it is this category of stalking that often results in long-term damage to the victim's reputation.

The intimacy-seeking stalker, often received as the rejected stalker, usually wants the same outcome as the rejected stalker—either the victims to come back to them or for their victims to be unhappy. In addition, these individuals will often utilize the online community to gain information about their targets such as their likes and dislikes prior to their first face-to-face meeting. However, in distinguishing between these two categories, with the intimacy-seeking stalker, there was no actual relationship (and perhaps minimal contact) between the two parties; thus, there is no relationship for return. Unfortunately, for many individuals, and especially teens, perception is reality. The teens that have perceived a relationship to exist when in fact it did not may engage in the stalking behavior for a longer period.[18] This is explained in part as, in their mind, they want to return to their memory of a perfect relationship. With adult stalkers in intimacy-seeking relationships, these relationships have the propensity to turn violent as with the case of Rebecca Schaeffer. In teen cases, many of these occur when a gay or lesbian teen perceives a heterosexual peer to be their "true love"; the actions most often include posting sexual messages, enrollments of their victims in homosexual chatrooms, and other aspects of cyberstalking. Also, included in teen cases of intimacy-seeking stalkers are teens that may not desire a sexual relationship with their victims but desire group membership in their victim's clique.[19] For some reason, they are not allowed to become members of that particular clique.[20] This category of stalker is obsessed with their victims and their victim's daily habits and routine.

The incompetent stalker is another category of stalkers and is quite common in the teen world. These are the individuals that, because of an inability to understand social protocol or a lack of social skills, simply desire to be a part of their victims' world and do not understand that their victims do not want to engage in a relationship (romantic or friendship) with their stalkers. For parents, this is probably the most disturbing, not from the child victim's perspective, but from the child stalker perspective.

No parents want to consider that someone may not want to be friends with their children. In some cases, with this category of stalker, parents will actually encourage their children to aggressively seek the attention of their victim. Unfortunately, as the incompetent stalker continues to pursue their person of interest in both the real and virtual worlds, their person of interest may react aggressively in the real and virtual world (cyberbullying).[21] The parents, who may have been concerned about the fact that their child may be stalking a peer, now might have the concern that their child is now the victim of cyberbullying in retaliation.

The resentful stalker, often associated with hate groups or actions of bias, is the individual who, because of some characteristics of the victim, decides to target a person because of some demographic of the victim. These stalkers are often encouraged by adults to follow and monitor certain individuals or groups of individuals for the purposes of reporting activities and locations of victims for other forms of abuse. The intent of these stalkers is damage to the person or their property. For example, one teen may vandalize another teen's car, post damaging statements about the person, or send constant unflattering text messages, because the victim is a tall blonde cheerleader and the stalker feels that they were denied the opportunity to be on the cheerleading squad because they were short and had red hair. In other cases, the stalker decides to target the victim because they perceive the victim as deserving of harassment—the individual is overweight, therefore deserves to have pictures of them eating in the cafeteria, at fast food restaurants, or eating in their car posted on a website for overeaters. Lastly, a victim may be stalked because of their membership in a racial, ethnic, religious, or homosexual group. If an individual's group affiliation is considered a threat or an annoyance because of an encounter or a bias, then that individual may become a victim of stalking or cyberstalking.

Finally, the predatory stalker, although not as common as one believes, is the type most likely to concern parents. These are the stalkers that target individuals for abuse. These are the individuals most thought to be perceived as the stranger lurking in the darkness, awaiting the opportunity to abuse their children. For parents, these were the individuals identified in the "stranger danger" campaigns and were most often the adult males in search of children to victimize. In terms of teens and cyberstalking, these cases are rare in that the predatory stalker's desired outcome is the physical abuse of their victim; thus, cyberstalking does not provide that end result. However, in cases involving child enticement and sexual exploitation through cyberspace and means such as child pornography, this category of stalking may exist in conjunction with the other ICAC.[22]

In the majority of stalking or cyberstalking cases, the stalker is known to their victim and most stalkers have had some degree of involvement in their victim's lives.[23] In considering the demographics of stalkers, parents should be aware of the fact that stalkers of adults are usually male; however, stalkers of teens are both male and female and, just as in the cases of cyberbullying, females are likely to be perpetrators of cyberstalking.[24] In fact, females are increasingly becoming identified as stalkers and cyberstalkers. An example of this action was demonstrated in 2011 in Seattle, Washington, when two preteen girls posted messages, and instant messaged random individuals under their victim's name to arrange sex acts. The preteen girls, at one time friends with their victim, used their victim's password and her Facebook page to facilitate their cyberstalking.

In July of 2011, a 12 year old Washington girl was convicted of cyberstalking and sentenced to probation and community service after she and her 11 year old peer altered the Facebook account of a classmate with explicit photos and solicitations for sex.[25]

Just as in cases of cyberbullying, the anonymity of the online world and cyberspace facilitates individuals and their abilities to cyberstalk their victims. Stalkers, and especially cyberstalkers, have no fear of repercussion.[26]

WHAT DO STALKERS DO?

Multiple actions and activities by perpetrators have been identified in cases of cyberstalking. Those factors include posting false information on websites or in chatrooms to damage a victim's reputation, approaching friends and family of the victim as well as monitoring the victim online to collect information on that victim, and virus attacks on the victim's computer. Other factors in cases of cyberstalking include the involvement of an "innocent" in the action through encouraging others to harass the victim, ordering services such as a pizza delivery in the victim's name, and false reports of harassment or victimization by the victim to local law enforcement. For child victims of cyberstalking, it is also not unusual for stalkers to attempt to arrange personal face-to-face meetings with their targets.[27]

Stalking, which can escalate over time to become more frequent and more violent, is usually exhibited by the stalker (or perpetrator) through common actions. Those actions include, but are not limited to, following their victim and being present at events that their victim would normally attend. Traditionally, stalkers often will send unwanted gifts, cards, or letters to their victims. Stalkers will drive by their victim's home or work, hire private investigators to follow or research their victim, and seek out friends or family members of their victims. Through cyberstalking, these actions are extended as victims now receive emails or text messages from their stalker or are the subject of online searches through public records.[28] In addition, cyberstalkers are often allowed to follow their victims through social media or electronic surveillance, and, in some cases, computers and financial accounts of victims are accessed by the cyberstalker.

Cyberstalkers utilize a variety of methods to monitor and harass their victims.[29] Specifically, email, text messages, newsgroups (a method of online communications where groups post their thoughts on a particular or dedicated topic such as how to victimize groups of individuals based upon some demographic characteristics such as homelessness), instant messaging, and Internet sites such as those advertising sexual services with the victim's contact information posted online. However, parents should be aware that most prosecuted cases of cyberstalking are not technically sophisticated.

In terms of destructive behaviors, traditional stalking included damage to a victim's home, automobile, or pets as well as threats of violence to the victim and the victim's family.[30] Cyberstalking extends those destructive behaviors to include not only those violent outcomes of traditional stalking but also damage to reputations through posts within the online community, damage to finances as bank accounts and credit applications may be accessed, and damage to computers and other remotely accessed electronic devices.

For the majority of stalkers and cyberstalkers, victims are subjected to multiple approaches or harassments within an average week. In addition, most cyberstalkers utilize multiple means of approach, both on- and offline. Finally, many stalkers and cyberstalkers have had victims prior to their current victim and some may return to a previous victim.

Again, for teen stalkers, actions most often involve cyberstalking.[31] A teen stalker may drive past the home or school of their victim, but they are also likely to be following their target through social media, attempting to contact their target through instant messaging, online postings, and email. In addition, applications such as Snapchat, Instagram, and Twitter allow teen cyberstalkers to maintain a connection with their victims. Finally, teen stalkers, because of their use of technology, are less likely to reveal themselves to their victims; hence, the stalking has the potential for continuing longer than traditional stalking encounters. Teen cyberstalkers rely on the ignorance of parents and the public to facilitate their efforts.[32]

WHAT DOES STALKING DO TO MY CHILD?

Most adult victims of stalking, and particularly those victims of long-term stalking, report escalated levels of fear. These victims are afraid of what actions their stalkers may take, they are fearful of placing themselves in vulnerable or isolated positions, and they are often fearful of trusting others. Teen victims of stalking are no different; however, given that much of the stalking of teen victims is through the online community, the effects may be worse for those teens. In particular, given that many teens today place a strong emphasis on their identity within the online community, victimization within this arena may lead to feelings of vulnerability, anxiousness, depression, and hopelessness for the teen victim.[33] In addition, the stress of victimization through cyberstalking may result in many teens displaying eating problems such as loss of appetite or anorexia, problems with sleeping, trouble in concentrating, and disturbing thoughts of self-injury. In fact, research suggests a significant relationship between being a victim of stalking and reports of severe depression.[34]

As parents of victims of stalking or cyberstalking, we must be aware of these behaviors demonstrated by our children. In some cases, because of embarrassment over an action or fear of judgment, our children may not come to us for help; therefore, the ability to recognize these symptoms of victimization is critical. For parents interested in additional information on stalking or cyberstalking, several groups exist to provide these resources. Specifically, the National Center for Victims of Crime supports a Stalking Resource Center. Another group is Working to Halt Online Abuse (WHOA) which is designed to educate the public on the subject of online harassment. Finally, Cyber Angels is a nonprofit group designed to provide assistance to victims of online harassment and cyberstalking. For many of our children, their feelings of defeat at the hands of an unknown opponent in cyberspace are very real and, in some very unfortunate occasions, cyberstalking is the beginning of a child's destruction.

IS MY CHILD A STALKER?

Stalking or cyberstalking behaviors may exist on a continuum of involvement. At a minimal level of involvement, actions by the stalker may be perceived as inappropriate or mildly intrusive. At the maximum level of involvement, actions are aggressive, persistent, and oftentimes destructive. As parents, we should not only recognize these behaviors to help protect our children from victimization, but also to help protect our children from being a perpetrator of stalking or cyberstalking. In these cases, parents should listen to their children. By focusing attention on their social likes and dislikes as well as the likes, dislikes, and actions by their peers, parents may be in an ideal position to identify behaviors that may be perceived as stalking or cyberstalking. Unfortunately, just as we as individuals are not always the best judge of our actions, we as parents are not always the best judge of our children's actions. The thoughts of "my child would never do this" or "my child simply became involved in the wrong group" are common among parents. However, interesting to consider is the fact that a parent's child may have become involved in the "wrong group" but rarely is it acknowledged by a parent that their child is the "bad seed" in the group. In cases where there exists the potential for your child to be the perpetrator of stalking or cyberstalking, a trusted friend or objective family member may be in a better position to identify the child as the stalker.

Parents must communicate the essential need for privacy to their children. Specifically, parents should explain to their children the importance of not providing online "friends" their physical location or their last name. In addition, if their teens have been involved in a destructive relationship, parents should encourage them to change their passwords in the event that a former boyfriend or girlfriend may know their password and gain access to their accounts. Finally, parents should encourage their teens not to accept invitations for conversation from individuals they do not know, to block anyone who demonstrates strange or aggressive behaviors toward them through their social networking sites, and to report to their parents any persistent and unwanted contacts.

HOW DO I PROTECT MY CHILD?

Given that stalking and cyberstalking are compulsive and obsessive ICAC, it is unlikely that these activities will end simply because the perpetrator has changed his or her mind. Hence, parents must take measures to protect their children before and if stalking or cyberstalking occurs. Of course, the easier way to address victimization is to eliminate its potential from the very beginning. Parents may be the resource to provide that information to their children.[35] Of course, not all victimization may be eliminated; however, through proactive measures, much of the risk for victimization may be reduced. Parents should provide rules and suggestions for their children and teens to be followed while they participate in the online community.

First, parents should assure that their teens remain off adult (starting at age eighteen) dating sites within the online community. In addition, if, after conversations between parents and their children, teens decide to participate in a teen dating site, parents should provide their children rules for conduct. Specifically, when engaging in online teen dating sites, parents should communicate that their teens are not to reveal personal information such as their last name, where they attend school, where they attend church, or where they live until they have met their online friend face-to-face.[36]

Second, parents should remind their teens of the dangers of having a camera on their bedroom computer or laptop. If a camera is included in these electronic devices, parents should assure that the cameras are covered when not in use and that their passwords are changed regularly to avoid individuals hacking into and controlling their systems.

Third, as with the case with other types of ICAC, parents should communicate to their teens the rule that not all friend requests should be accepted. If they do not know the person placing the friend request, then the request is denied. Fourth, for security reasons, parents should enforce the mandatory rule that passwords on all of their teens' social networks and apps be changed regularly and that passwords are not shared with anyone other than the parent.[37] Fifth, parents should communicate to their children that, under no circumstances, do they post, tweet, or discuss where they are going, when they are away from home, and their current physical locations. Finally, parents must monitor their teens' existence within the online community and must periodically check on their teens' activities while online in cyberspace.

If parents discover that their children or teens are victim of stalking or cyberstalking, parents must report the abuse to their local law enforcement community.[38] In addition, parents must mandate that their children cease to continue with their online and cell phone accounts and, if necessary, initiate new accounts within the online community.

SUMMARY

By definition, stalking and cyberstalking involve a consistent action. Parents must recognize these consistent actions by their children if they are to help prevent their children from becoming the perpetrator. In defense of the children, sometimes teen relationships and the ending of teen relationships are confusing to all of the parties involved. For one person, there may be a hopefulness of reconciliation; for another there may exist only the intent to remain cordial. Mixed signals and changes in moods and desires provide an excellent environment for teen cases of stalking and cyberstalking. However, if the parents notice a persistent attempt to telephone, text, or instant message another by their child and perceive the action as unwanted by the intended recipient, parents should recognize the action. In addition, if parents notice their children following, surveilling, or sending unwanted or unaccepted gifts to another, they should be aware of these characteristics of stalking. Finally, if parents suspect that their children are destroying the property of another, spreading rumors about another, or threatening to harm another, they should intervene if in no other way than to talk to their child about the actions of stalking and cyberstalking and the inappropriateness of their actions toward another.

In 1990, California was the first state to enact antistalking legislation. Since that time, all fifty states and the District of Columbia have enacted laws against stalking; however, most stalking laws at the state level continue to require credible threats of violence toward a victim by an offender. In 1994, the federally sponsored Violence against Women Act was signed as a part of the Violent Crime Control and Law Enforcement Act to provide funds to support the investigation and prosecution of violent crimes against women. In 1996, the Interstate Stalking Act made it illegal for someone to cross state boundaries (physically travel) with the intent to injure or harass another person. In 1998, President Clinton signed the Online Child Protection Act which made it a federal crime to use any form of interstate commerce such as the telephone or the Internet to solicit or entice a child into illegal activities. Finally, during this last decade, legislative actions such as the 2013 Violence against Women Act have been revised and rewritten to include stalking or cyberstalking.

Again, cyberstalking is the use of technology to facilitate stalking and is a very real concern for parents. Teens who spend much of their time online (as increased online time is related to increased risk of victimization) face a substantial risk for victimization through cyberstalking. Teen victims of stalking report escalated levels of fear. These victims are afraid of what actions their stalkers may take, they are fearful of placing themselves in vulnerable or isolated positions, and they are often fearful of trusting others. In addition, teen victims of stalking, who place a strong emphasis on their identity within the online community, report feelings of vulnerability, anxiousness, depression, and hopelessness. In addition, the stress of victimization through cyberstalking may result in many teens displaying eating problems such as loss of appetite or anorexia, problems with sleeping, trouble in concentrating, and disturbing thoughts of self-injury. As a parent, the protection of our children is just as essential in cases of stalking and cyberstalking as it is with other ICAC.

Chapter Seven

Facilitating Hate and Violence

Linda often cleans her seventeen-year-old son Marc's bedroom while he is in school. One day she notices KKK symbols in his room as well as racial and religious slurs posted across his computer's screen saver. When he returns home, she asks him about the materials she has found and is stunned at his comments regarding white supremacy. She asks him his source of information and he introduces her to what she perceives to be a forum dedicated to hate and destruction.

At least one protest occurred monthly in the United States during 2015. The subjects of those projects included worker-employer conflicts, racial inequality, and police officer-involved shootings. The overwhelming majority of these events were peaceful and nonconfrontational. However, some were not as some resulted in arrests, violence, and even deaths. Our First Amendment provides all citizens of the United States the right to gather, protest, and to speak. This protection of speech is one of the most covenanted rights afforded in our country and is not available to many living outside of the United States.

First Amendment: United States Constitution (Abridged)

Congress shall make no law respecting an establishment of religion, or prohibiting the free exercise thereof; or abridging the freedom of speech, or of the press; or of the right of the people to assembly, and to petition the Government for a redress of grievances.

It is also the protection most referenced in discussions on free speech, posts on the subjects of hate and violence via the Internet, on social blogs, and through social networks all within cyberspace.[1] Unfortunately, many of our children and, in particular, our teens, find these posts to be interesting and appealing. It is these electronic posts that often attempt to facilitate bias and hate in our society and it is these posts that should be a concern to parents. These actions, not traditionally classified as ICAC, are attempts by some individuals to involve our children in crimes of bias and hate against others or child corruption. For clarity, child corruption as presented in this chapter is the encouragement of a minor to commit an illegal offense against another or another's property.[2] For this chapter, the result of child corruption is demonstrated in actions of violence or property destruction as influenced by perceptions of bias and hate. Hence, these actions attempt to involve our children in illegal activities.

> In July of 2015 a 21-year-old white male was charged with federal hate crimes adding to the multiple state counts of murder which resulted from a South Carolina church shooting on June 17th. In 2016 Dylann Roof is convicted of the deadly shooting spree which resulted in the deaths of nine African American church attendees.[3]

The Southern Poverty Law Center (SPLC) is a nonprofit organization located in Montgomery, Alabama, which was founded in 1972 to monitor hate groups and other extremists within the United States. The state of Alabama is a reasonable location for this nationally recognized center as Birmingham in the 1960s was the location for the beginning of a series of sit-ins, marches, and boycotts to protest the segregation laws in the South. According to the SPLC, there are over eight hundred active hate groups and hundreds of extremist groups existing today within the United States. Many of these group members post messages and recruit new members via the Internet and cyberspace. It is these groups that should be of concern to any parent as it is these groups that actively recruit teens into their organizations with the intent of involving new members in actions of destruction. As young adults and teens are prime targets for recruitment, parents, once again, are in the best positions to reduce this outcome.

As parents, we all know that the teenage years are a time in which individuals are seeking a sense of identity or group attachments by which to belong. Today's hate groups recognize this "search of self" by young people and often utilize the online community to facilitate the exposure of their ideas to this impressionable audience. As parents, we must have some knowledge of those groups that attempt to influence our children's thoughts and actions. We must also be aware that, although many groups and organizations are not created to facilitate hate and destruction, members of some of these groups utilize these connections and cyberspace to incite violence by its members.

HATE CRIMES

The majority of hate crimes are nonviolent offenses such as the vandalism of property.[4] When a hate crime is violent, it is most often an assault or threats of violence against one person. Hence, the classification of a hate crime is not based upon the criminal action but rather the intent behind the action.[5]

Approximately 20 percent of hate crimes in the United States occur within the school setting or on a college campus.[6] Approximately half of all hate crimes are outcomes of bias based upon either race or ethnicity. Approximately 25 percent are outcomes of bias based upon religion, and approximately 25 percent of hate crimes are based upon a bias toward sexual orientation.[7]

When considering the perpetrators of hate crimes, the majority are under the age of twenty-five with nearly 30 percent of those individuals under the age of 18.[8] Hence, teens are actively involved in actions of hate which include not only the destruction of property but also the victimization of individuals. Finally, the majority of the perpetrators of all hate crimes are young males.[9] Therefore, given this propensity of hate or extremist groups to involve our children, parents must be knowledgeable on the subject of hate.

Through a variety of posts, discussions on various topics of bias and hate occur every day within the online community. As parents attempting to protect our children from crimes involving the Internet, we must understand that not all ICAC are active sexual crimes and that some forms of enticement (or persuasion) may involve encouraging actions of destruction. Therefore, parents must also be aware of groups that exist and attempt to recruit our children into acting upon their philosophies of hate and sometimes violence toward other groups or individuals.[10] In these cases of ICAC, the child or teen may not be the target of the actual victimization, but is the target for recruitment in participating in victimization. Although not normally considered by parents in the protection of their children, these ICAC may produce severe long-term effects on children and even more damage to society as a whole.

Five such groups or movements that may or may not be classified as a hate group and may have been originally organized as peaceful are: (1) Anarchist, (2) Black Lives Matter, (3) Ku Klux Klan, (4) Nation of Islam, and (5) New Black Panthers. Members of these groups, who practice the First Amendment rights, should not be of concern to parents. However, in all of these groups, there have been incidents by a small minority of the group's members that have participated in acts of violence and destruction. It is these extremist members that should be of concern to the parents of teenagers. However, prior to discussions on some of today's more popular groups or movements popularized within cyberspace, parents should first understand the manifestations of hate and how hate groups operate to forward their goals. By understanding the process, parents may be able to intervene to prevent their children's corruption and participation in hate crimes against others.

EXPLAINING HATE

The outcomes of hate in history are legendary with the obvious results of mass destruction and mass murder. However, when one begins to explain why another hates something or someone, the rationale becomes less apparent.[11] Attempts to combat hate or thoughts of hatred is limited and, in many cases, ignored as how does one objectively end an action with subjective, philosophically based dynamics?

Hate is divided into two categories: rational and irrational.[12] Rational hate results from acts perceived as unjust. Irrational hate is demonstrated as a hatred of a demographic or behavioral characteristic of a person of groups of people (i.e., sex, race) often without the experience of personalized victimization.

In explaining rational hate, the focus by the perpetrator (i.e., hater) is usually the unjust action performed against them or another within their inner circle and their inability to effect change or their own perceived helplessness to prevent the victimization. In these cases, an individual is abused by another and feels hate toward their abuser. For example, a young male assaults a young female; hence, the young female, as well as her family and friends, may hate that particular male. In other cases, a person or group may be the target of hate when the hater perceives that they have suffered as a result of their target's action. For example, a female may be promoted within an organization and her male colleague may hate her because, in his mind, he did not receive the promotion because the leaders of the organization gave her the job because "she is a woman." In this case, the male hates that individual female who was promoted, but not all women. Thus, the female is the target of the male's hatred. For many, although this is classified as rational hate, it should be acknowledged that it is a result of the victim's perceived outcome and not necessarily the intent to victimize by the "offender."

Irrational hate, the category of hate involving most actions of mass destruction, is much more difficult to understand. Some suggest, just as the notion of the Cycle of Violence in child abuse,[13] that this behavior or philosophy is passed down from generation to generation as a learned behavior. It is also this category of hate that rarely results from a personal account of abuse or victimization by the target of hate. Irrational hate is often displayed in off-color jokes about certain races, genders, or religions or in actions of discrimination toward individuals based upon their appearance. For example, the burning of a cross in the yard of an African American home simply because of the race of the homeowner is a demonstration of irrational hate. Hence, irrational hate allows the hater, most often a very insecure individual, to elevate themselves above their hated subject. From this vantage point, the hated individual is perceived as less worthy and, therefore, deserving of the bias, discrimination and, eventually, hate. It is this category of irrational hate that fuels the memberships and actions of those involved in hate group or groups that facilitate hate and destruction against others.

MODEL OF HATE[14]

Hate is not a spontaneous act. We are not born hating others. It is a learned behavior with, as many have suggested, a process of steps and stages. In particular, the psychopathology of hate groups suggests a seven-stage model of hate. Through each stage or step, the hatred of a group is identified, solidified, and acted upon. From a sociological perspective, one might consider this a "collective behavior" as individuals come together for an action. From a psychological perspective, one might consider this a "power of individuals" in that one charismatic person can influence the actions of others. Regardless of the perspective, through the stages of this model, the outcome for many individuals is victimization.

It is suggested that in the first stage of the Hate Model, haters, who rarely desire to hate alone, are motivated or driven to gather as individuals into a common group. Our notion of *strength or protection in numbers* is demonstrated in this behavior. Individuals, and particularly teens, who are unwilling to demonstrate actions of destruction alone, are more likely to participate in these actions if acting in a group.

In the second stage, the group begins to form its own identify through the bonds of common thoughts, meanings, or ideas. It is also during this stage that symbols or rituals are introduced as well as mythologies, goals, and the mission of the group. Just as is often demonstrated in religious practices, human beings are often uncertain or at a loss when it comes to faith. For many of us, that means that to believe in something, we must visualize or even to touch a symbol of our faith. In the Hebrew Bible or Old Testament, this was demonstrated over and over again and was apparent in the story of Moses leaving his followers only to later return to discover them worshipping a golden calf. Just as that known story illustrates the need for individuals to (for lack of a better phrase) have something to see before they could believe and follow, symbols or rituals attract and support followers in hate groups, and are often necessary especially given our young generation which has been raised with visual stimuli such as PowerPoint presentations in the educational setting.

The third stage in the hate model is established to specifically identify the person, persons, object, objects, or organization for hatred. It is during this stage that we, as group members, know exactly who we should hate, even if we do not know why we hate them. The famous story of Romeo and Juliet demonstrates this stage as the members of the two families do not like each other; however, little or no explanation is provided on the reasons for this disliking or hatred.

During the fourth stage, the hate group verbally targets the foci of hate. This stage is demonstrated in racial slurs, negative stories, or demeaning jokes that somehow lessen the perceived value by group members of the target. It is during this stage that members use the N-word to address those of African American descent, the *fag* word to address those in the homosexual community, the phrase *Camel Jockey* for individuals of Middle Eastern descent, or the phrase *Christ Killer* for a person of the Jewish faith.

During the fifth stage, the haters move from verbal abuse to physical abuse or the destruction of property. It is during this stage that we see the vandalism of buildings, the burning of structures, and physical assaults against individuals. It is during this stage that reports are often made to law enforcement; however, in the teen community, these forms of abuse (referred to as bullying) are not reported until the actions become consistent and severe.

During the sixth stage, the hate group attacks the target or targets with weapons. These weapons may include not only baseball bats and firearms, but also poisons and explosives. It is during this stage that the destruction of property and the severity of injury are significant. In addition, law enforcement or emergency services officials are involved in reaction to the attacks.

In the final (or seventh) stage, the hate group destroys the target. Fortunately, this seventh stage of the hate model is an extremely rare occurrence. However, parents should be aware of these stages of hate to better protect their children from themselves becoming a perpetrator of hate.

GROUPS AND MOVEMENTS

The following is a discussion on common groups or movements in today's society. It is acknowledged that not all of the groups discussed facilitate hate; however, the perception of some in society is that they do facilitate anger and violence toward targeted groups. Thus, for informational purposes, parents should be aware of the background and mission in all such groups or movements.

Anarchist

The Circle A is today's most common symbol for anarchy. The symbol is simple—a capital letter "A" surrounded by the capital letter "O." The letter A stands for Anarchy and the letter O stands for Order. In general, anarchy refers to the support for antigovernment control. For adults this might mean no restriction or laws by our government regarding living conditions, gun ownerships, or marital restrictions. For teens, antigovernment control could mean not only antigovernment but also, since their most prominent forms of regulation are the school setting, hence, antischool restrictions. It is these antischool philosophies that most concern parents in the wake of bullying, harassment, and other forms of violence, all within the school environment. Parents must recognize the influence to *fight the system* that so boldly is portrayed by this group and is often appealing to teens within the online community. When considering that teen involvement in hate crimes is common and that over 20 percent of hate crimes occur within an educational setting, parents must acknowledge the potential for this type of ICAC.

Although today's current symbol for anarchy existed prior to 1965, the punk-rock movement of the 1970s helped to popularize and facilitate its use. Originally, this symbol was associated with the Federal Council of Spain and the International Workers' Association; however, few know of this origin.

In 1886, in Chicago, the symbol first began its association with violence in the Haymarket Affair or Haymarket Massacre, which began as a peaceful protest for workers' rights and turned into a violent encounter as explosives were thrown into the crowd resulting in the deaths of seven police officers and four civilians. In the legal proceedings which followed, eight anarchists (i.e., members of the group) were convicted of crimes associated with, and including, murder. These convictions for violence and the media's attention to the event increased the public's interest in the organization.

To further illustrate the violence perceived to exist within anarchism, in the early 1970s, *The Anarchist Cookbook* was first published. This book contained antigovernment messages as well as instructions on how to manufacture explosives and some forms of illegal drugs. After reports of the book being used in violent actions to include school shootings nearly two decades later, the book was refused reclassification by the Office of Film and Literature Classification and banned from publications in various countries. However, in 2012, a revised *Cookbook* was again published in America. The *Anarchist Cookbook* has also helped to increase the popularity of this group and is an attractive read for many teens.

Today, this anarchist symbol is often used as a sensationalized marketing ploy with the intent to associated antigovernment or anarchist movements with chaos. These groups utilize the online community to spread their messages. In September of 2011, Occupy Wall Street in New York City was the name given to the protest against the wealthy, inequalities, and corporate government influences. These protests took the forms of picketing, demonstrations, and Internet activism.

For teens, the anarchist symbol is often perceived as fashionable—sold on t-shirts, dresses, and hats. It portrays the wearer as a "rule breaker," a rebel, or someone "cooler" than they perceive themselves. As parents, we should recognize this symbol when displayed by our children if only to be aware of its underlying premise and to educate our teen on the sometimes unfortunate outcomes that result from anti-establishment philosophies and the associations with those acts of destruction that are sometimes displayed by members of this organization. Although this group is not classified as a hate group, some individuals have aligned themselves with memberships in this group in order to facilitate their hatred toward individuals or organizations.

#BlackLivesMatter

Just as is the case with the previous group discussed, Black Lives Matter is not recognized as a hate group. Instead, it is an internationally recognized movement that began in 2013 as a nonviolent action through the hashtag #BlackLivesMatter after the Florida acquittal of George Zimmerman in the shooting death of African American teenager Trayvon Martin.[15] This hashtag, originally started by three women, gained in popularity and recognition the following year after two more African American males were killed by law enforcement officers. Again, #BlackLivesMatter is not a hate group but rather a movement, which presents itself in the most visible form (protests). In addition, Black Lives Matter was recognized as a runner-up in *Time Magazine*'s 2015 Person of the Year with over one thousand peaceful assemblies in the United States and globally since its inception.

This movement, intended to bring to society's attention the deaths of African Americans at the hands of police, has become one of the most powerful tools in social media for awareness of the vulnerabilities in many African American communities. Members of this movement have suggested the need for accountability and transparency in the criminal justice system as well as training for law enforcement in communicating with individuals of color. Unfortunately, some individuals (i.e., extremists) operating under the umbrella of the movement, are now accused of recruiting and encouraging individuals (and in particular young individuals) to harm and even kill law enforcement officers. In response, the Black Lives Matter movement has resulted in a White Lives Matter reactionary hate group (as identified by the SPLC). In a nutshell, a movement designed to bring people together for discussions, solutions, and harmony in race relations, is now used by some individuals wishing to promote hate and violence against law enforcement officers throughout the world.

> In September of 2016 a Dallas Police Sergeant filed a federal lawsuit against Black Lives Matter leaders and suggested that the July 7th murders of five Dallas police officers by Micah Johnson was encouraged in a Black Lives Matter demonstration.[16]

Just as with other groups, for many adults and teens, Black Lives Matter brings individuals together who desire equality and justice for all. However, for a few individuals, it is used as the basis for violent reactions either against police, who they claim victimize minorities, or by nonmovement members against members of the Black Lives Matter movement as a way to demonstrate white supremacy. As a parent, it is our responsibility to help educate and protect our children from such messages and actions of hate.

Ku Klux Klan

The Klan or Ku Klux Klan (KKK) is one of the oldest hate groups in the United States to advocate for white supremacy, anti-Semitism, and anti-immigration. The Klan, originally gaining popularity in the 1860s in the southern United States, was suppressed through federal legislation a decade later. At that time, KKK members, dressed in white robes and masks that hid their identities, attacked and intimidated African Americans, vandalized their property, and attacked those white individuals perceived as sympathizers or friends to African Americans all under the cover of darkness. Although stereotyped as only a group against the African American community and unfamiliar to many, around 1920, the Klan resurfaced in opposition to Catholics and Jews in the West and Midwestern United States.

Today's manifestation of the KKK emerged around the 1960s with their focus against the civil rights movement. The KKK, using the tactics of violence and murder to suppress individuals, is classified as a hate group. As of 2016, the SPLC reported a publicly recognized KKK membership of roughly six thousand US citizens. As a parent, we all have grown up hearing stories of the KKK (especially those with families in the South); however, in this technological age, the image of individuals dressed in white robes and burning crosses in the yards of African Americans may not be an accurate depiction of the activities.

In April of 2016, two white teens were arrested for sending a video of a hanging and threats to do the same to an African American student via Snapchat.[17]

Today, the fastest growing communications media for the messages and recruitment jargon of hate groups is the Internet. It is through these sophisticated online recruiters that leader cells of bias and hate are created within the outer edges of the organization. Through the Internet, hate groups such as the KKK have found a cost-effective way to reach and attract a younger and wider audience.[18] These efforts, for the most part, work as memberships and groups such as the KKK continue to flourish.

Finally, for teens and many adults, the KKK is known as the ultimate in white supremacy groups. Over the last decade with the controversies surrounding the Confederate flags in the southern United States, the KKK has been active in the protests of Confederate flag removals from government buildings through the rationale of culture and the protection of Southern heritage. For teens searching for group membership that is recognized to "preserve history" and the culture of slavery, the KKK is an attractive organization. Parents must communicate to their children not only the historical significance of the KKK, but also today's messages of hate under the association of the KKK within cyberspace.

Nation of Islam

The Nation of Islam (NOI) is an African American Islamic Religious Movement founded in Detroit, Michigan, in the 1930s. The stated goals of the NOI are to improve the spiritual, mental, and economic conditions of African Americans in the United States. However, critics suggest the organization is essentially a black supremacist organization although it was not originally identified as a hate group by the SPLC. The NOI's current leader (since 1977) is Louis Farrakhan, who is headquartered in Chicago, Illinois. Key leaders for NOI were Elijah Muhammad, who called for a separate nation for black Americans and for the adoption of a religion based on the belief that blacks were God's chosen people, and Malcolm X, before his conversion to Orthodox Islam. The slogan for NOI is "Justice or Else."

Today's leaders of NOI have repeatedly denied charges of anti-Semitism. They do, however, maintain the supremacy of the black man and discourage interracial marriages. The NOI has been listed as a recognized hate group by the SPLC since 1998. For teens looking for a group to belong to, the NOI actively recruits young men and provides a large congregation of over twenty-five thousand members within the United States. Teens interested in NOI membership become what are called a "Fruit of Islam" from the ages of fourteen to twenty-five. After the age of twenty-five, they become members of the NOI. Unfortunately, some individuals, under the umbrella of NOI promote violence against non–African Americans. For teens who are easily persuaded into bias and hate, parents must be aware of the fact that there is the potential for the promotion of violence by some members of NOI.

New Black Panthers

The Black Panthers (or the Black Panther Party for Self-Defense) was an African American socialist organization founded in the 1960s to support black communities in the United States and remained active until the early 1980s. However, as violence from the Black Panthers increased, memberships decreased as individuals within this organization began seeking nonviolent and more successful resolutions. As a result, the New Black Panther Party was founded in the late 1980s and has called for a separate black nation.[19] It should be acknowledged that current known members of this group were not members of the original Black Panthers Party and that the majority of the original members have publicly disassociated themselves from this new group.

The SPLC describes the New Black Panthers as a hate group with anti-Semitic undertones and who encourages violence against whites and law enforcement officers through media assaults on the KKK and law enforcement with the intent to incite hatred. For a young person looking for group membership, the New Black Panthers provides a purpose by publicly celebrating (online) the man who killed five Dallas police officers of 2016 and issuing a call for violent gangs across the nation to continue the attacks against law enforcement officers.

For teens seeking a cause with biases toward whites, law enforcement, or Jewish individuals, the New Black Panther Party provides the excitement and rush of action as well as the potential for danger. In addition, the symbol for the New Black Panthers, similar to the symbol for the Carolina Panthers football team, is appealing to young people seeking a popular image for clothes and other novelties. Again, parents, it is our duty to recognize the symbols of such groups to better converse on these subjects and better protect our children. It is also our duty to recognize the influence of cyberspace in facilitating this form of child corruption.

HATE CRIME LEGISLATION

For nearly five decades, the United States has attempted to reduce crimes based upon bias. The first federal effort to address hate in the United States was the 1968 Civil Rights Act which permitted the federal prosecution of anyone who willingly injures or intimidates a person because of their race, color, religion, or national origin.

In 1990, the US Congress signed the Hate Crime Statistics Act into law. Before this act, hate crimes existed but were not tracked or provided identity as a specific category of crime. The FBI, not utilizing the term "hate," defines a "crime of bias" as a criminal offense committed against a person or property or society which is motivated, in whole or in part, by the offender's bias against a religion, race, disability, sexual orientation, or ethnicity/national origin.

In 1994, the Violence against Women Act allowed victims of a gender-motivated hate crime to seek relief. Also in 1994, the Violent Crime Control Act increased the federal penalties for hate crimes on the basis of race, color, religion, national origin, ethnicity, or gender. In addition, the 1996, Church Arson Prevention Act was enacted to protect against the burning of churches based upon the racial composition of their parishioners.

Finally, in 2009, as a result of two cases of murder based upon hate, the Matthew Shepard and James Byrd Jr. Hate Crime Prevention Act extended the categories of federal hate crimes to include crimes motivated by bias based upon perceived gender, sexual orientation, or a disability.

In September of 2016 in New York, a 14 year old was arrested for a crime of bias after he set fire to the clothes of a woman dressed in traditional Muslim attire as she walked down the street.[20]

Today, many states have also adopted anti-hate laws, which vary by type of bias. However, most address bias based upon race or ethnicity and none of the states has recognized the use of cyberspace.[21] As of July 2016, forty-five states prohibit crimes motivated by bias based upon race, religion, and ethnicity, thirty-one states prohibit crimes motivated by bias based upon sexual orientation, thirty-one states prohibit crimes motivated by bias based upon gender, seventeen states prohibit bias crimes based upon gender identity, twenty-three states prohibit bias crimes based upon disability, and twenty-two states prohibit crimes of bias based upon age or political affiliation. For states without laws specifically prohibiting crimes of bias, individuals may also be charged for a crime of bias at the federal level in addition to their state-identified crime.

PROTECTING MY CHILD FROM HATE

In the United States, it is not illegal to have a bias toward or a hate for a group of individuals. However, it is illegal to destroy a person's property or commit an act of violence against that person because of the victim's demographic or behavioral characteristics. In other words, it is not the thought that it is illegal, but rather it is the action of destruction that is illegal for crimes of bias.

As parents, it is our duty to protect our children from committing actions toward others based upon hate. In addition, the majority of the victims of hate crimes are under the age of twenty-five and many are teens. Of those young victims, most are male and most are victimized as a result of a sexual-orientation bias. In all of these cases, the victims are someone's children.

The first step in that protection, after awareness of the various groups, is the control of perceptions. For many individuals, including teens, perception is reality. What a teenager views in cyberspace or reads on Facebook or Instagram may be perceived as true by the teen. In other words, a five-second clip on YouTube or a picture on Snapchat may attempt to represent a real-world situation. As adults, we know that a five-second video does not explain (or show) the events that occurred before the action. As parents, we understand that one picture does not show the details of the event. However, teens may not have that understanding of reality. It is the responsibility of us as parents to provide our teen the opportunity for questions and dialogue on such topics bias and hate.

In addressing the issues of bias and hate with your teen, parents should understand that as teens, they will express their own ideas and opinions. For many teens, those ideas may not match those of their parents. From a parent's perspective, the goal is communication, not conflict. Hence, your reactions to their statements are critical. In a nutshell, the more dramatic your reaction as a parent, the more likely your conversation with your teen will end. Therefore, parents must listen and allow their children to express their thoughts on the subject. An important strategy for parents is to plan multiple conversations on the topic within brief periods of time to allow not only for their children to process the discussions, but to also allow the parent an opportunity to gather their thoughts and control their emotions as related to the topic.

Finally, it is also critical to remember that for many young people, perceptions are not only taken from the online community and cyberspace, but also from the words and actions of their parents and peers. As parents, we cannot control the actions of our children's peers; however, as adults, we should control our own statements and actions. Thus, as parents, one of the best ways to protect our children from ICAC that attempt to recruit them into actions of violence against others is to model the behaviors that we feel appropriate for a civilized society of respect.[22]

SUMMARY

Unfortunately, hate is a very real part of our society. In response, legal efforts to reduce crimes of bias or hate have existed for decades. In today's society of technology, the use of the online community by individuals interested in recruiting individuals for participation in their actions of hate and destruction is not uncommon. The most commonly recruited individuals are young people, to include teenagers. Hence, child corruption is also an ICAC that should be of concern to parents.

As parents, we all know that the teenage years are the time in which individuals are seeking a sense of identity and hate groups recognize this "search of self" by young people and will often utilize the online community to facilitate the exposure of their ideas to this impressionable audience. As parents, we must communicate to our children that, although many groups and organizations are not created to facilitate hate and destruction, members of some of these groups utilize these connections and cyberspace to incite violence and destruction by its members.

Parents wishing to protect their children from these very unique types of ICAC must be aware of the individuals, extremist group members, and efforts that exist today to facilitate destruction. By modeling behaviors of acceptance and peace as well as communicating with their children on the subjects of bias and hate, parents may be able to prevent the recruitment of their children into the extreme activities which result in the harm and fear of others.

Chapter Eight

Preparing for the Worst

Sex Rings, Sex Tourism, and Child Trafficking

Donna is a single parent with three children ages seven to fifteen. Her oldest daughter Tamara, who is always asking her for money, now seems to have a constant supply of cash to purchase not only clothes but also fast food for the family. One day, Donna notices that Tamara has a new cell phone. When she asks her daughter where it came from she claims to have purchased it with money given to her by a friend. Donna does not know this friend but does notice that Tamara will often leave home for a couple of hours after receiving text messages in the evenings.

With the 2009 release of the film *Taken*, which starred Liam Neeson as a father whose daughter is abducted for victimization by the sex trade, the idea of victims of sex rings, sex tourism, and human trafficking became an issue of concern for parents and the public.[1] Until the film, many assumed that only through stranger kidnappings were children forced into the sex industry. However, once the film was released, the notion of teens being coerced or tricked by someone they know into participating in the sex industry became a worry for many parents. With the increased use of electronic postings, chatrooms, and dating apps to facilitate these types of crimes, the idea that their child or teen may be a victim of this most severe category of ICAC became very real for many parents. In this chapter, for the purpose of discussions and, with the potential outcome of death for its victims, sex rings, sex tourism, and child trafficking are all considered severe categories of ICAC.[2] In addition, this chapter provides information to parents in terms of legal reactions to these severe forms of child exploitation as well as on explaining these concepts and actions to their children.

111

Child abuse, for the most part, is considered intimate and personal;[3] however, child abuse through the sex trade is considered cold, revenue-generating, and global.[4] With transportation means as they exist today, children and particularly teens are easily moved (transported) from location to location or country to country. This ease of mobility facilitates the likelihood of their involvement in the illegal trades of sex rings, sex tourism, and child trafficking.

For clarity, a child sex ring (hereafter sex ring) involves one or more offenders,[5] usually adult males, who are simultaneously sexually involved with several child victims at one time. These children can be both male and female, of a variety of ethnic and racial backgrounds, and, while most are teens or preteens, many are as young as preschoolers or infants.

Sex tourism, another avenue in the sex trade, entails adult individuals engaging in both national and international travel to participate in sexual activities considered to be illegal and unethical in those individuals' respective countries of residence.[6] In these cases, typically adult males visit other countries to engage in sex with very young girls or boys. In sex tourism, the consequences of the constant travel by offenders and child victims, who are moved throughout an area to provide variety for their clients, results in extremely difficult illegal activities to detect by law enforcement and other governmental officials. In this most severe form of ICAC, the organizer of the sex ring as well as the clients are considered perpetrators of child sexual abuse.

Finally, human trafficking is defined as the recruitment, transfer, harboring, or receipt of persons by threat or use of force.[7] Critical to this definition are the elements of force or threat of force to coerce the actions of movement and criminal behaviors which exist. In other words, human trafficking involves movement and actions without the consent of the victim.[8]

Child trafficking is often misidentified as child smuggling and, although the smuggling of individuals continues to be a growing problem in the United States, trafficking is a distinct activity which involves exploitation. Interpol defines smuggling as the illegal act of enabling the entry of a person into a state for which that person is not a permanent resident. With smuggling, the move is always transnational and, once the individual reaches their desired geographic destination, their relationship with their smuggler is terminated. This is not the case with human trafficking as if the victim is denied their freedom of movement or to change employment once moved into an area or if the consent of the victim to leave one country for another was through coercion or deception, then human trafficking has occurred. Hence, some cases of smuggling may become cases of human trafficking but cases of human trafficking are not simply cases of smuggling.[9] Therefore, sex rings, sex tourism, and child trafficking are all of concern for parents dedicated to the protection of their children. In many cases, over the last decade, these severe crimes are facilitated by the use of the Internet and cyberspace.

> During 2015, in FBI arrested approximately 150 adults who operated a child sex ring involving over 100 children in US cities such as Alexandria (VA), Cleveland (OH), Denver (CO), Detroit (MI), Los Angeles (CA), and Seattle (WA). The majority of those offenders arrested were convicted. Most of those child victims were teens or preteens and were US citizens.[10]

The child sex trade does not affect most children and the majority of those children are from outside of the United States. In fact, it is suggested that only a fraction of approximately 1 percent of the children in the world are victims; however, in worst case scenarios, a child, even a child in the United States, may become a victim of the sex trade. Therefore, there are children at risk for these forms of abuse.[11] In general, most child victims in the sex trade are also victims of childhood neglect and, neglect is the most common form of child abuse in the United States. Hence, actions which were thought to exist outside US borders may now exist within the United States and parents should be aware of these occurrences.[12]

SEVERE INTERNET CRIMES AGAINST CHILDREN

The sex trade and specifically, the trafficking of children, has recently become recognized as one of the most profitable criminal enterprises that exists today. This enterprise involves the maltreatment of children and generates millions of dollars on an annual basis. Estimates suggest that traffickers can receive a 2,000 percent profit through the exploitation of just one young child.[13] This criminal enterprise involves children, who are simply viewed as a product worthy of victimization for profit. Thus, adult human trafficking and child trafficking is a very lucrative illegal business which is expected to continue until it ceases to be profitable, which is unlikely.

Many individuals who are victims of human trafficking are exploited or trafficked for one of two reasons: sex or labor.[14] Both reasons victimize men, women, and children. Children are also trafficked for those reasons in addition to sex and labor. These reasons include adoption, for drug smuggling, and for their healthy organs (i.e., liver, lungs, and kidneys).

Incidents of sexual victimization and human trafficking have existed for generations; however, it is suggested that child victimization through the sex trade has become more prevalent in developed countries with the fall of communism in the 1980s and was then facilitated by the technology age that occurred shortly after that same time.[15] The overwhelming presence of poverty, job insecurity, and an inadequate education system created a favorable environment throughout Europe for child sexual exploitation; however, in the United States, with an abundance of poverty, drug-addicted parents, child throwaways, and teens utilizing the online community for all things social, the increase of opportunity for those types of criminal victimizations has led to the reality of child victims within US borders.[16] Hence, it is not difficult to imagine with this form of ICAC. Nationally, parents must be aware of this potential danger in order that their children remain safe. Current annual reports produced by the US Department of State suggest that child sex rings, sex tourism, and child trafficking cases continue to increase with approximately twenty thousand victims detected in the United States every year.[17] The average age of these US victims is between twelve and thirteen.[18]

Cases of child sexual exploitation through sex rings, sex tourism, and child trafficking are often identified in reports of human trafficking. Specific information on the young victim is limited; however, most child victims were provided an avenue into the criminal victimization through someone known to them. The Department of State has estimated that there have been over 150,000 sex slaves identified within the United States since 2001,[19] and many of these victims were under the age of eighteen. This age demographic for these types of ICAC are often younger than child victims of solicitation or pornography and, for many of these victims (nationally and internationally), parents or other family members are aware of their sexual exploitation.[20]

Historically, information and assertions about adult victims of human trafficking have been applied to child victims in regard to the number of children, the dynamics behind the victimization, and the perpetrators; however, recent research suggests that these assumptions may not be true and that technology may play even a larger role in the victimization of children for these severe crimes than in the victimization of adults. Victims are identified and perpetrators are contacted, in the majority of the cases, via the online community or a cell phone.

LEGAL ACTIONS

During the twentieth century, there was no single agency responsible for the collection of information or data on sex rings, sex tourism, and human trafficking and there was little interest in the activity even though in 2000 President Bill Clinton signed the Trafficking Victims Protection Act (TVPA) to prevent these forms of sexual exploitation. However, after Secretary of State Colin Powell announced that monies acquired through human trafficking helped to support the 9/11 hijackers while they lived in Florida,[21] the public and the government began to recognize the prevalence of this criminal activity and initiated combative efforts to reduce not only the victims but also the perpetrators of these severe forms of sexual abuse. Also, during that time, legal attention was received on the domestic slave trade within the United States and intracountry efforts were initiated through nongovernmental organizations (NGOs) in the United States and worldwide to provide resources to those identified as victims.

In 2002, President George W. Bush signed an executive order to establish an Interagency Task Force charged with strengthening efforts among agencies and identifying the needs of victims of trafficking and other forms of sexual exploitation while punishing offenders and preventing future victimization. The TVPA was amended and signed in 2003 as the Trafficking Victims Protection Reauthorization Act (TVPRA), which mandated responsibilities and duties for federal agencies in addressing human trafficking and victimization. It was also established with the 2000 TVPA and the 2003 TVPRA that the Office to Monitor and Combat Trafficking Persons exist as an Interagency Task Force to strengthen and coordinate efforts among other criminal justice agencies and to assist in the identification of the needs and services for trafficking victims.

In 2003, the United States strengthened its role in fighting human trafficking and other severe forms of sexual abuse by passing legislation specifically to address child sex rings and child sex tourism. This legislation, the Prosecutorial Remedies and Other Tools to end the Exploitation of Children Today (PROTECT) Act, was adopted to seek and punish aggressively those Americans involved in traveling to participate in sex tourism and child sex rings.[22] This measure, along with the various states passing laws against forced child labor and child sexual exploitation, demonstrated the commitment by the United States to end the severe abuse of child sexual exploitation. Finally, in 2014 the Preventing Sex Trafficking and Strengthening Families Act acknowledged the use of cyberspace in these crimes and strengthened support for victims' services once these cases are discovered.

Today, in most states, convicted traffickers face a minimum sentence of twenty-five years in prison. Individuals convicted of participating in child sex tours and child sex rings may also be imprisoned. However, day after day in the United States and abroad, one case after another is discovered involving severe sexual exploitation and a child. In 2015, the State Department suggested that the number of victims involved in any form of child sexual exploitation has doubled since 2012 and that there are between 200,000 and 350,000 at-risk children in the United States on an annual basis. These estimates average to approximately seven hundred child victims of sexual exploitation per day. Children within the United States are targeted through cyberspace by friends already being victimized, at a neutral location (such as a shopping mall), and through cell phone communications with individuals identified as "recruiters" in the sex industry.[23] Parents are normally unaware of these potential risks to their children.

WHY CHILDREN ARE EXPLOITED

For parents to begin to understand why children would be victims of sexual exploitation, they must first eliminate from their mind the concept of a child as a person and view the child as a product, a product worthy of much effort in its care and very profitable to its owner—in fact, a single child victim may produce over $250,000 per year for their abuser.[24] From the perspective that the child is the product, the individual wishing to sexually abuse the child is considered the consumer, and the perpetrator is the means of recruitment, production, and distribution for the product. The sexual victimization of a child is simply the outcome of the consumer's desire. Therefore, from a rational, objective, perspective, child sexual exploitation is a business. It is a business that we, as parents, want to prohibit in the recruiting and victimization of our children.

First, in considering child sex rings, usually within the category of extrafamilial (outside the family) abuse, multiple children and multiple abusers are involved. Through this type of exploitation, there is sexual activity among multiple child victims and multiple adult offenders. Traditionally, in child sex rings, there are communications (often online) among the offenders in terms of the desired demographic characteristics of a child such as the age and gender of the child and the sex ringleader's ability to identify and locate a sought-after child. Historically, this line of communication involved either a phone or email. Today, communications among offenders may still occur through phone lines and email; however, they are much more likely to occur in private chat rooms, instant apps, and websites operated as "discussion-only" forums from computer servers based outside the United States, therefore, outside US regulations. These forums, self-identified as discussion-only for individuals to share their thoughts on sexual activity, lead to members moving to more private venues for sharing images and videos of child pornography as well as their plans for participation in a sex ring to abuse children.[25] Hence, this ICAC operates without police knowledge, without police jurisdiction, and without intervention. In 2011, an international Internet-based child sex ring with over seventy thousand members and over two hundred children in thirty countries (to include the United States) was uncovered by EUROPOL (Europe's international law enforcement agency). With multiple law enforcement jurisdictions, varying laws, and few children identified by name, the prosecution of those responsible is extremely difficult and, therefore, an ongoing investigation.[26]

Second, in considering the child victims of sex tourism (or as our government defines it—the extraterritorial sexual exploitation of children), federal law prohibits any US citizen from traveling to a foreign country with the intent to engage in any form of sexual conduct with a minor as well as to help organize or assist another person in traveling for this purpose. However, each year Americans are convicted of committing this crime and, in 2005, the convictions of a pediatrician, a dentist, and a university professor by the US government helped to dismiss the idea that those involved in these types of crimes were poor, uneducated, and feared criminals.[27]

Historically, three of the most popular destinations for sex tourism are the countries of Thailand, Brazil, and Spain.[28] These are also countries which are often locations for educationally based study-abroad trips for American high school and college students. Advertising for these child victims is found online through classified ad sites such as Craig's List, Backpage, and various dark net sites. For clarity, the term "dark net" refers to a network that requires special access and is characterized by the anonymity of users and hosts to conceal illegal activities such as the production and distribution of illegal drugs, hidden financial accounts, or illegal sexual activities. To avoid detection and facilitate child abuse, most dark net users utilize code words related to ordinary objects such as food to discuss the desired characteristics of children. For example, the food item of pasta may represent a *young boy* and the food item of *pizza* may represent a *young girl*.

Unfortunately, the relative ease and automation of international travel in today's society has led to an increase in this type of ICAC. Some suggest that individuals who seek to sexually abuse children desire this category of sexual abuse and some suggest that, because this crime most often occurs outside of US boundaries, that Americans, who would never sexually abuse a child in the United States, are drawn to this crime because of the anonymity that comes with being in a foreign country.

In a nutshell, technological advances have revolutionized the travel industry and, as a result, the Internet has helped to facilitate information on the locations of child victims for sexual abuse.[29] Therefore, parents should be aware that, although most assume the child victims of sex tourism are international children, there are American victims as these tours also exist within the United States. Finally, with the ease of international travel from the United States, their child could become a victim in another country.

Finally, in considering child trafficking, one must acknowledge that children are trafficked for a variety of reasons in addition to sex and labor. Specifically, children are trafficked for: labor, adoption, drug smuggling, sex, for healthy internal organs, and, in some countries, soldiering and camel jockeying. Each use of a trafficked child equates to profit to his or her trafficker. In addition, as the child is moved when necessary for abuse by the paying consumer, there rarely exists an opportunity for the detection of the victimization by an individual outside of the organized criminal unit. Cyberspace and the online community will often facilitate this illegal activity as commercial sex purchasers will, in many cases, browse the Internet to select children for trafficking or for involvement in either sex rings or child sex tourism.

Over the last decade, the adoption of trafficked children has been recognized by several governmental and NGOs.[30] Specifically, government officials are recognizing the involvement of organized crime in these adoptions. These crime organizations provide infants to desperate couples seeking to adopt a child. The traffickers involved in this type of child trafficking typically purchase the desired babies from the mother or father in need of money. These parents may live within the United States or outside of the United States. The most babies in the United States are white Americans or of white European descent. As couples in the United States are willing to pay more than $30,000 for a baby, the demand is always present. The traffickers will identify possible children or babies on the basis of their physical characteristics and often utilize the Internet to facilitate the exchange. Again, one must consider the child as a product, individuals willing to pay any price for their desired product, and the trafficker as the distributor to understand the dynamics of this crime and the risk for some infants.

Children are also trafficking as "drug mules" for use in the smuggling of drugs. Historically, adult men and even women who appeared to be pregnant were used to transport drugs, particularly from Mexico and South America, into the United States; however, as security measures have increased and the searching of baggage and persons has become more prevalent in airports and land-border crossings, individuals, including children, are commonly transporting drugs by means of ingestion. Children, from a trafficker's perspective, are excellent hosts for ingesting drugs for the movement of drugs across borders as the children often do not receive the scrutiny of customs or immigration officials when they enter the country accompanied by an adult (usually a female). If the small bag of drugs that is swallowed by the child dissolves or leaks into the stomach of the child, then death is a common outcome. However, as the child is viewed as cheap, disposable, and easy to replace, the trafficker in-volved in drug smuggling suffers less of a financial loss with a child than with an adult. In these cases, another child is quickly obtained and then used as a replacement to continue the trade of drug smuggling.

Of course, the most commonly offered explanation for the human traf-ficking of women is sex trafficking, and sexual abuse is also the most common reason for the trafficking of children (both male and female).[31] Included within the reasons for the sex trafficking of children are child pornography, child prostitution, sex rings, molestation, the supporting sex tourism industry, and nude dancing. As sex involving children is supported by the human desires for gratification and profit, it is neither a phenomenon easily remedied nor an activity easily identified or inves-tigated by law enforcement. Sexual exploitation remains at the core for child trafficking with many children victimized through multiple actions of sexual abuse.

Finally, another reason for the trafficking of children is the desire for healthy human organs.[32] With the ever-pressing need for organs for trans-plantation in the United States and other developed countries, and this need fueled by the fear of AIDS in adults, a child is the perfect victim of human trafficking for internal organs. The child's organs are more likely to be healthy and HIV negative; therefore, it is very profitable for those involved in trafficking and for those not against murdering a child for profit. Of course, many of the conversations and connections regarding organ identification and transportation occur within the online commu-nity. Again, the Internet and its reach among American citizens and these individuals living outside of the United States should be of concern to parents wishing to reduce or end the trafficking of children.

HOW DOES CYBERSPACE FACILITATE THESE ICAC?

Child victims of sexual exploitation are not a homogeneous group. In fact, variations in terms of gender, class, race, age, nationality, and im-migration status are related to demand, their cost, and the amount of risk their perpetrators are willing to take. The tracking or identification of a child victim, once he or she begins the shuffle or mobility associated with sexual exploitation in the United States or any country, is nearly impossible. These child victims are often unable to speak English or the country's native language and are unable to seek help from law enforcement; therefore, they are subjected to repeated victimization.

The sexual exploitation of children in these severe categories of ICAC, with perhaps the exception of trafficking for adoption, is essentially a financial investment for their perpetrator. Parents should consider the three elements of any crime: a likely target, a motivated offender, and a lack of capable guardians. Unfortunately, in cases of child abuse, there will always exist motivated offenders or those who desire to sexually abuse a child. However, by reducing the likelihood of their children becoming targets and maintaining capable guardians in the supervision of their children, parents can reduce the cases of these most severe forms of child abuse.

Again, a single child can earn perpetrators thousands of dollars, and, if more children are exploited, the profits only increase. However, in identifying a child to be victimized, the location of the child as well as the family background of the child must be considered in addition to their physical characteristics. In the United States, the children or targets who fall prey to sex rings, sex tourism, and trafficking are often runaways, immigrants, refugees, children in foster care or neglected children (also called throwaways). In actuality, less than 5 percent of US child victims are kidnapped and restrained. Just as is suggested in research on the abuse of children by family members and strangers, opportunity for abuse must exist. Unfortunately, the Internet often provides that avenue of opportunity.

Parents should be aware in cases of child sexual abuse, the abuse is not at the hands of a stranger. Just as with traditional cases of child sexual abuse, there exists a process of identification, recruitment, and grooming prior to victimization. In a traditional manner, a perpetrator would see a child, begin interacting with the child, gain that child's trust, then victimize the child. In these types of ICAC, the child is often involved in the online community and therefore is easily identified by the perpetrators. As discussed previously, perpetrators may (under the anonymity of the online world) represent themselves as another teen or the child/teen may initiate the interaction with the perpetrator while knowing that the perpetrator is an adult (often a young male adult). Through conversations within the online community, the child victim interacts with the perpetrator.[33] Eventually, the child and the perpetrator arrange a face-to-face meeting. The opportunity for sexual exploitation has been presented. Parents must be aware of this process to better protect their children.

Finally, parents or caregivers may both serve as capable guardians over their children. Unfortunately, as the teen years emerge, parents are less likely to monitor the activities or mobility of their children. This lack of supervision, and sometimes supervisory neglect, for teens and preteens helps to explain the overrepresentation of this age cohort in these forms of abuse.[34] Parents must be aware of and active within their preteens' and teens' world in order to maintain the safety of their children from individuals seeking unsupervised youths for victimization.

WHAT CAN PARENTS DO?

The growth of child pornography is one explanation for the increase in child sexual exploitation. Online child pornography fuels the demand for child victims, sex rings, sex tourism, and trafficking are all gateways to the victims of these types of sexual exploitation. As it becomes easier to identify and contact children via the Internet, it becomes easier for those interested in the exploitation of children to identify a potential victim. However, parents can help to prevent these most severe forms of ICAC. Parents should be on the watch for the possible recruitment of their child into the sex industry. This *recruitment* may be observed in adults showing a special interest in their child, providing their children excessive or inappropriate gifts, or their children (teens) expressing a romantic interest in a young or middle-aged adult.[35]

Parents should also be aware of signs that someone may be *grooming* their children for the sex industry.[36] By observing their children becoming isolated from their family or friends they have had for years, by noticing their children expressing an interest in modeling or having their pictures taken by individuals, or by suspecting drug or alcohol use by their children, an individual may be attempting to groom their children for the sex industry.

Finally, parents should be aware of the *seasoning* of their children for the sex industry.[37] If parents notice signs of physical abuse such as bruises or burns, or signs of sexual abuse such as STDs or UTIs, an interest in sex education, as well as their children answering to names other than their own, they should be concerned. In addition, parents should be aware of brandings or tattoos that appear on their children. These tattoos or even brandings are signs of ownership and if a child or teen is tattooed, it is not only acknowledged to the sex industry that the child is available for abuse, but in many ways it is psychologically acknowledged by the child that they are the possession of another without the option of free will afforded to all citizens of the United States.

In Virginia in 2015, a 21 year old man was convicted of the tattooing and sexual abuse of two girls, each under the age of 13 while serving as their babysitter. In addition to his convictions, the mother of the girls and her boyfriend were also both convicted on charges of child abuse and sentenced to more than one year in prison for their roles in the incidents.[38]

As with any case of ICAC, communication with your child is essential. This communication includes not only information of preventive methods to reduce their likelihood of their child/teen contacting a perpetrator but also the communication of information on cases of victimization that have occurred within their area or to a victim with demographics similar to their own (i.e., sex or age). If these conversations occur regularly, and in different venues such as car rides or during dinner, children and teens are more likely to listen, and at least be cautious in their conversation with individuals within the online community.

IF MY CHILD IS A VICTIM?

If parents suspect that their children are victims of one of these severe forms of ICAC, law enforcement must be contacted immediately. By reporting the suspected victimization to law enforcement, two actions result. First, law enforcement officials may begin their investigation into the potential case of victimization and the criminal justice process becomes the lead in the process of justice. Second, by reporting the victimization, the teen or victim is alerted that the parent or parents will be there to help and protect them, and, in most cases, the parent will also be there for their teens as they recover. Several nonprofit organizations in the United States are dedicated to ending these severe forms of child abuse.

Specifically, Polaris Project, named after the North Star that helped to guide some of southern slaves to freedom in the 1800s, located in Washington, D.C., is a group formed in 2002 to fight human trafficking. This organization, which attempts to disrupt human trafficking networks, also works with victims as well as lobbies elected officials for strong legislative actions to prevent human trafficking. Another organization, Hope for Justice, established in 2007, has offices in Tennessee, London, Norway, and Cambodia and was also created to combat human trafficking by helping to rescue victims and improve awareness. In addition, there are international efforts to address these severe forms of ICAC. One such effort is Interpol's Special Group on Crimes against Children, which was formed in 1992 to assist with victim identification and to serve as a resource for law enforcement training.

This element of acceptance and support is essential for victims of any form of sexual abuse, but particularly those child victims of severe sexual abuse. By parents, acknowledging the victimization of their children also are helping to assure their children that they are not in the position of blame, but in the position for help.

SUMMARY

The sex trade and the severe forms of child sexual abuse have been recognized as some of the most severe forms of ICAC. In addition, the sex trade has been recognized as one of the most profitable forms of criminal enterprise. Again, with the release of the 2009 film *Taken*, the idea of child victims of sex rings, sex tourism, and human trafficking became an issue of concern for American parents and the public and, once the film was released, the notion of teens and preteens being coerced or tricked by someone they know into participating in the sex industry became a worry for many parents. Legislative actions to reduce these severe forms of ICAC include the 2000 Trafficking Victims Protection Act (TVPA) to prevent these forms of sexual exploitation, the 2003 Trafficking Victims Protection Reauthorization Act (TVPRA), which mandated responsibilities and duties for federal agencies in addressing human trafficking and victimization, the 2003 Prosecutorial Remedies and Other Tools to end the Exploitation of Children Today (PROTECT) Act, and the 2014 the

Preventing Sex Trafficking and Strengthening Families Act acknowledged the use of cyberspace in these crimes and strengthened support for victims' services once these cases are discovered.

For American citizens, it is often comforting to acknowledge that the children in the United States are safe. However, this may not be the case. Whereas the majority of America's children are not victims of these severe forms of sexual abuse to include sex rings, sex tourism, and child trafficking, there are cases of all of these categories of sexual exploitation in the United States and all have included American children. The parents' job is to protect their children from these forms of abuse.

Unfortunately, due to connections within the online community, the Internet is a major facilitator for these forms of ICAC. From the parents' perspective, the protection of their children must be considered regardless of the limited risk to American children. As with all ICAC, parents must be involved in the lives of their children, must be aware of their friends and social networks, and must know who they are communicating with in the online community.

Chapter Nine

Warning Signs

In nearly every case of child sexual abuse, the community members, teachers, and peers are surprised and shocked that the victimization of a child has occurred. The initial responses about the victim and sometimes the perpetrator are often that both were wonderful people, well liked, hard-working, a delight to be around, and an important contributors to the community. However, afterward, there are some individuals who, upon thinking about the abuse, proclaim that there were warning signs or indicators that the victimization was occurring.[1] Unfortunately, in some cases, these indicators were only recognized when the consequences of the abuse to the child were fatal. From a parent's perspective, warning signs must be recognized if the ultimate goal is the protection of their child.

As the various ICAC have been identified throughout this book, this chapter provides parents a summary of the physical as well as behavioral indicators that may exist if their child is a victim of an ICAC. As the majority of the ICAC are related to sexual exploitation and sexual abuse, many of the indicators of ICAC are the same as those for traditional cases of child sexual abuse. For ease in the organization of this chapter, the physical indicators for ICAC will be identified followed by the behavioral indicators by type of ICAC. In addition, this chapter will provide a discussion on the safeguards that have been proposed by experts in the field of ICAC as well as information on the process of reporting ICAC to law enforcement and specific information that parents may provide to law enforcement officials to aid them in their investigations.

WHAT ARE THE SIGNS THAT
MY CHILD IS A VICTIM?

In very few cases of child victimization do there exist clear-cut signs of abuse or exploitation; ICAC are no different.[2] With ICAC, there are also not always specific signs of abuse. Parents who regularly observe and interact with their children are often the best individuals to identify change in actions and behaviors by their children, which may be in reaction to abuse or exploitation.[3] The following are suggestions for parents to note and are not intended to be a specific list of the signs and symptoms of ICAC; however, they are signs and symptoms for recognition. Again, for most parents, the key to identifying victimization is in noticing the change in the behaviors of their children.

Physical Indicators of ICAC

In cases of ICAC, the majority of the abuse is or is related to sexual exploitation.[4] Hence, in most of these cases, just as in traditional cases of child sexual abuse, there are no physical indicators (or evidence) of the abuse. The two reasons for this lack of evidence are: (1) the child was not sexually assaulted by another; and (2) the abuse was not reported immediately, therefore, any sort of physical evidence has either been washed away or has healed.[5] However, there are some physical indicators of ICAC which may be present with the child victim.

The first physical indicator, if collected immediately after an assault, is physical evidence such as blood, scrapes, cuts, bruises, semen, saliva, and remnants of lubricants.[6] Again, this aspect of physical evidence must be collected immediately for its best use. With this form of physical evidence, the child testimony may not be required.

The second physical indicator of an ICAC is the presence of a sexually transmitted disease (STD) or a urinary tract infection (UTI).[7] These are especially significant in cases of severe violence with teens and preteens, who are victims of abuse by multiple partners. In addition, this is especially important in cases of very young (i.e., under the age of thirteen) victims.

The third physical indicator of an ICAC is a teen's or preteen's preoccupation with touching his or her genital areas.[8] This preoccupation may be in reaction to an itching or burning in the genital areas as well as an action of pleasure revealed through their participation in an ICAC. For the very young victims, this touching for pleasure is most likely a behavior revealed to them by their abuser.

The fourth physical indicator of an ICAC is self-abuse by a teen or preteen.[9] Hence, evidence of self-mutilation, anorexia, bulimia, and attempts at suicide may all be indicators of victimization through an ICAC. Unfortunately, self-abuse is often a long-term consequence of abuse. For parents, noticing the physical indicators of self-harm, in most cases, the child has been abused on multiple occasions over periods of time.

Finally, a fifth physical indicator of an ICAC, which is also present in many traditional cases of child sexual abuse and often overlooked, is the hygiene of the child.[10] Specifically, children who are victims of sexual abuse and ICAC will often attempt to make themselves less attractive to perpetrators by not bathing, not brushing their hair, and not brushing their teeth. This is especially the case for very young children or for children who are developmentally delayed. Unfortunately, long-term consequences of these behaviors include not only medical infections but also dental problems, which may continue well past their time of victimization.

However, with ICAC, where there exist no physical indicators (again in the majority of the cases), parents must be aware of the behavioral indicators in order to protect their children. Some of those behavioral signs or indicators are provided below as related to the specific ICAC as a guide for parents.

Behavioral Indicators

The parents' desire is to be there and help their children when needed. Unfortunately, with ICAC, many children, because of their perceptions of involvement and self-blame, will not ask their parents for help.[11] Hence, parents must be the ones to initiate questions to their children on abuse. These questions may be the result of a parent's observations of specific behaviors by their child.

Enticement, Sexual Imposition, Child Solicitation, and Child Pornography

As suggested, often a victim of ICAC will provide hints of that abuse or exploitation through behavioral indicators instead of the physical indicators.

In general, these child victims may experience problems in school, problems with authority (to include parents), be comfortable with the use of sexual language or descriptions of sexual acts, and either be extremely aggressive or extremely submissive in their interactions with peers.[12]

Parents should be aware that in cases of child exploitation through enticement, child solicitation, and child pornography, many children will display behavioral indicators similar to traditional victims of sexual abuse.[13] Therefore, just as victims of traditional child sexual abuse, teen and preteen victims of ICAC are often withdrawn from their family and offline community. Reasons for this withdrawal are usually related to embarrassment for being lured into these categories of ICAC or fear of parents and others knowing about their sexual activities which at any time could become very public. In addition, these victims spend much of their time online and alone. Finally, victims of these types of ICAC are often secretive about their communications and will often close or minimize their computer screens if another person enters their room or work area when they are online or have many phone numbers in the cell phone's contact list with new numbers being added on a regular basis.[14]

Sexting and Sextortion

Children and teens are involved in sexting for a variety of reasons; however, for the most part, older teens are more likely to sext when compared to preteens. Unfortunately, children in their preteens have been known to not only receive but also voluntarily send messages or images to others of a sexual nature. Parents, who are unaware of the practice of sexting in the teen community, are not likely to be the first individuals to notice their children's or teens' involvement in sexting. However, if parents are able to recognize certain behaviors, they may be able to limit the child's involvement in sexting.

First parents must recognize that for most teens, the thought of their peers involved in sexting is not something that they would consider inappropriate or surprising. Reasons for teen involvement in sexting often mirror the reasons provided by adults for the same action; the teen is involved in a sexual relationship or they are interested in a new partner and want to provide that newly desired person a sexual conversation or image as a flirtation. However, because of their age, the teens who are the perpetrator of sexting, is also distributing child pornography.

Second, parents should be aware that solicitations for images from others are also a reason for teen sexting, which in extreme cases may lead to sextortion.[15] With mass media representations of the perfect human body, teens often place enormous pressures on themselves in terms of physical appearance. Females, who may be proud of their appearance in certain sexually suggestive clothing, may sext others as an attempt to receive attention or compliments regarding their appearance. Males, with the pressure to have a large erected penis, may sext pictures of their genitalia.

Finally, victims of sextortion may demonstrate some of the same behavioral indicators as those involved in sexting; however, as sextortion is essentially electronic blackmail, victims of sextortion have reported immense signs of psychological stress such as anxiousness, nervousness, and trouble sleeping.[16] In addition, victims of sextortion often choose to be alone and often avoid leaving the safety of their homes.

Thus, for parents, the question of whether their children or teens are the victim or perpetrator of sexting is often answered with—yes, to both. Teens and preteens, because of their willingness in many cases to send sexually explicit narratives or images, in some cases discover that their private "message" is now public. Hence, the teen initiator (or perpetrator) of sexting is now the victim of sexting, and perhaps a victim of sextortion.

Cyberbullying

Even with the best of preventive measures, some children will be victims of cyberbullying and, as a parent, you should acknowledge the fact that your child may be that victim. If you feel as though your child is a victim of bullying or cyberbullying, you should ask them. Keep in mind that for many teens reporting victimization by peers is embarrassing, even reporting the abuse to your parents. It acknowledges that they are not liked by a peer and that, in some cases, they are disliked by their peers.

For a parent, the reaction to this report by the child is critical. Practice your "game face." When your children or teens report to you being a victim of cyberbullying—listen, do not react or criticize, and do not offer the quick advice of "just stand up to your bully." Unfortunately, in some cases of cyberbullying, the teens may not know the identity of their bully and if the teens suspect an individual to be their cyberbully, they still may not want a confrontation with that person. If the case exists where your teenager does not know the identity (or identities) of their cyberbully, however, the bullying language references activities within the school environment, then you (or your teen) should contact the guidance counselor within the school to report the bullying.[17] Most schools have in place antibullying policies that apply to these situations and through discussions with the other students, the guidance counselors are often able to identify the perpetrators of cyberbullying. By identifying the perpetrator of cyberbullying, their anonymity is nonexistent; hence, the cover of the online community is greatly reduced. In addition, guidance counselors are trained in mediation and, in many cases, resolve the conflicts between students. If your teenagers do not know the identity of their cyberbully and messages appear in which activities outside of the school environment are referenced, then you, as a parent, should seek answers within that venue (e.g., if youth activities with a church are referenced within the online messages, then the parent should speak with church youth leaders to help identify the source).

Specific signs of cyberbullying that parents may notice include the appearance of uncomfortableness by the child when they receive a text message or email as well as a desire by their child to not attend school or other outside the home events.[18] In addition, victims of cyberbullying will often refuse to share any details about their online community and may become angry if asked. Other behavioral indicators of victimization via cyberbullying include depression, withdrawal from family and friends, and trouble sleeping.[19] Also, stress-related symptoms such as headaches, stomachaches, and weight gain or loss may indicate cyberbullying. Finally, as discussed early in this book, self-harm or threats of suicide are also potential outcomes of cyberbullying and strong behavioral indicators to parents that something is happening with or to their child.[20]

Cyberstalking

Most adult victims of stalking report escalated levels of fear. These victims are afraid of what actions their stalkers may take, they are fearful of placing themselves in vulnerable or isolated positions, and they are often fearful of trusting others. Teen victims of stalking are not different.[21] In fact, given that much of the stalking of teen victims is through the online community, the effects may be worse for those teens. In particular, given that many teens today place a strong emphasis on their identity within the online community, victimization within this arena may lead to feelings of vulnerability, anxiousness, depression, and hopelessness for the teen victims. In addition, the stress of victimization through cyberstalking (similar to the stress of cyberbullying) may result in many teens displaying eating problems such as loss of appetite or anorexia, problems with sleeping, trouble in concentrating, and disturbing thoughts of self-injury. As parents of a victim of stalking or cyberstalking, we must be aware of these behaviors demonstrated by our children. For many of our children, their feelings of defeat at the hands of an unknown opponent are very real and, in some very unfortunate occasions, cyberstalking is the beginning of a child's self-destruction.[22]

Child Corruption

For many parents the thought that their children are active in aggressions of hate toward an individual or groups of individuals is inconceivable. However, parents must be aware that there are individuals within the online community who wish to recruit their children for acts of destruction. In these cases, parents must be aware of the behavioral indicators that often exist before acts of violence or destruction.[23]

These indicators, similar to the indicators displayed by teens and preteens prior to incidents of school violence, include: poor academic achievement, disciplinary problems, difficulties with family or peers, a history of family and/or peer violence, the perception that aggression is normal, involvement with alcohol and/or drugs, access to firearms or other types of explosives, and the claim that they have "been wronged" by an individual or groups of individuals.[24]

Severe ICAC

Although few parents will ever experience the victimization of their children via a sex ring, sex tourism, or trafficking, there are indicators of these types of victimization that parents should note in case these incidents occur. Specifically, victims of these severe forms of ICAC will often report multiple boyfriends or one particular boyfriend and multiples of his friends. In addition, victims of these types of ICAC may have money in addition to their money provided to them by their parents or a part-time job.[25] Victims of sex rings, sex tourism, and child trafficking may also be fearful of law enforcement or other authority figures.[26] They are often in the company of an adult (usually a young male adult) but rarely speak for themselves. In addition, these victims often lose track of time and, when asked about their activities, are vague with responses.[27] Finally, victims of these severe forms of ICAC usually do poorly in school, are often seen in sexually provocative clothing, and utilize drugs and/or alcohol.[28]

HOW DO I PROTECT MY CHILD?

The sexual abuse of children is among the most horrifying and disturbing category of child abuse. From the media's perspective, the sexual abuse of a child is front-page news. Unfortunately, of the four categories of child abuse, sexual abuse was the last to receive public attention and demand for reaction.[29]

Historically, the sexual abuse of anyone was not a subject for discussion. The sexual abuse of children was even less likely to be discussed and, if the perpetrator was a family member, which was often the case, the subject was taboo. Today, the sexual abuse of children is recognized as a crime against innocence and of public concern as well as a topic worthy of discussions, prevention, and legislative action.

As referenced, in 2013, over six hundred thousand children were confirmed victims of child abuse in the United States. Of those cases, approximately 10 percent were victims of child sexual abuse.[30]

The information presented in this chapter on child victims and their offenders is based upon known victims of child sexual abuse. However, many incidents of child sexual abuse remain unreported. In fact, when comparing general rates of adult rape reported to law enforcement through the Uniform Crime Reports (UCR) and those reported on victimization surveys through the National Crime Victimization Survey (NCVS), it is estimated that only about one-third of the crimes are reported to law enforcement.

Given the facts that young children are often unable to report their abuse, that many of their abusers are family members, and that family matters are still intensely private,[31] it is suggested that child sexual abuse is even more underreported than adult cases of sexual abuse.[32] In addition, and as if child sexual abuse is not damaging on its own, current research on the prevalence of child sexual assaults indicates that incidents of child sexual abuse over the last decade have become significantly more violent and, in many cases, end with the death of a child.

There are no clear indicators of risk for child sexual abuse.[33] Children from all ages and all backgrounds are victims; however, some research suggest some factors increase risk. Specifically, research suggests that social isolation of the child or family is a major contributor.[34] Others suggest that children's cultural background is a significant risk factor in their risk for abuse, domestic violence is a risk factor for child sexual abuse, and that victimization is often simply a result of opportunity.

Children who are victims of sexual abuse within the family are, in most reported cases, females. However, in the cases of ICAC such as child sex rings, child pornography, and child trafficking, offenders are likely to be outside of the family and victims are often males.[35]

In considering ICAC and those offenders outside of the family, these abusers who target children often do so under the context of a social relationship with the child in either reality or cyberspace. These adults create special circumstances to place themselves in the proximity of children. Surprising to many people and contrary to the notion of "stranger danger" is that less than 50 percent of the cases of child sexual assaults are outside of the family; however, with ICAC, many of these offenders are identified as sex addicts, pedophiles, child molesters, individuals involved in child pornography, individuals involved in child sex rings, or individuals involved in child trafficking.

The sex addict, similar to drug addicts, adopts a delusional thought process to rationalize their behaviors. These individuals, preoccupied with the thought of sex, plan the abuse and then execute the plan, even though the victim is a child. Sex addicts are dominated by compulsive thoughts of sex and sexual activity.[36] Over time, just as with drug addicts, the sex addict must engage in riskier sexual activities such as with a child to produce the feeling of euphoria they most desire. Although research is conflicted on whether true sex addicts actually exist, reports suggest that approximately 70 percent of child molesters are labeled sex addicts.[37]

In addition, pedophilia is the sexual attraction to prepubescent children; however, it is not a crime to be a pedophile as pedophilia only becomes a crime when the offender acts on the desire for sexual activity with a child. One particular type of pedophilia is pederasty; this refers to the sexual activity of anal intercourse and is often with a boy.[38] It should be noted however that juveniles are more likely to commit sodomy compared to adults.

Pedophiles who targeted young boys outside of the home committed the greatest number of crimes with each offender reporting an average of over 150 child victims.[39] Individuals who target children via cyberspace also are likely to victimize many other children or teens before detected. In comparison, the situational pedophile may use force or another tactic to obtain sexual abuse as the current situation has provided the opportunity for abuse. The dependence of children often creates these opportunities for abuse.

Although illegal across the country, the production and distribution of child pornography is another type of sexual abuse. Through cyberspace and improved technology, the cases of child pornography have multiplied over the years. In these cases, sex offenders use the privacy of the Internet to identify those vulnerable children who use the Internet unsupervised.

In some cases of child sexual exploitation in cyberspace, adults coerce or manipulate children to pose or perform sexual acts.[40] In today's advancing technological environment, images of children may be digitally transformed into pornographic materials, and many of the children who appear in the electronically distributed pornography may never realize that they have been victimized. In these cases of child pornography, the children are victimized during the production of the pornography and then are repeatedly victimized as the pornography is distributed to the hundreds of viewers with Internet access and in search for child pornography.

The use of a cell phone to send sexual graphics or pictures as a form of romantic interaction is considered sexting, which is now very popular in teen relationships.[41] A teen sexting a nude picture of themselves to a romantic partner is no different from an adult sending a nude picture of a teen. Legally, in many states both actions are considered the distribution of child pornography. Young individuals involved in sexting may not realize they are producing or distributing child pornography. In fact, some estimates on the transmission of child pornography suggest that approximately 40 percent of today's child pornography originated with the child sending the picture to a peer. Unfortunately, once the teen releases the picture on the web, there is no point of return. The pornography is available for all with access to view, download, and redistribute.

Another type of extrafamilial sexual abuse involves the use of child sex rings.[42] The term sex ring refers to the situation in which one or more offenders are simultaneously involved in the sexual abuse of several children and the operation of a sex ring brings a different set of dynamics to child sexual abuse when compared to the "typical" familiar or extrafamiliar case of child sexual abuse. Finally, defined by the US Department of State as severe human trafficking, child trafficking is one of the most profitable criminal enterprises around the world today. Children across the globe are trafficked for a variety reasons to include sex.

As with all categories of ICAC, supervision and communication at a very young age are essential for protecting our children. In addition, parents should explain to their children throughout all stages of their development, the fact that individuals attempting to elicit a conversation with them while within the online community may or may not have their best interests in mind. Finally, parents should be mindful of the physical and behavioral indicators displayed by victims of ICAC.

Just as we have traditionally taught our children to beware of strangers attempting to approach them or talk to them, we must now caution our children about online approaches. Friends who attempt to converse with our children within the online community without parental consent, and particularly, friends from the online community who attempt to meet our children are to be avoided and are not really friends.[43]

First, parents should assure that their teens remain off adult (age eighteen plus) dating sites within the online community. In addition, if, after conversations between parents and their children, teens decide to participate in a teen dating site, parents should provide their children rules for conduct. Specifically, when engaging in online teen dating sites, parents should communicate that their teens are not to reveal personal information such as their last name, where they attend school, where they attend church, or where they live until they have met their online friend face-to-face.[44]

Second, parents should remind their teens of the dangers of having a camera on their bedroom computer or laptop.[45] If a camera is included in these electronic devices, parents should assure that the cameras are covered when not in use and that their teens' passwords are changed regularly to avoid individuals hacking into and controlling their systems.

Third, as with the case with other types of ICAC, parents should communicate to their teens the rule that not all friend requests should be accepted. If they do not know the person placing the friend request, then the request is denied. Fourth, for security reasons, parents should enforce the mandatory rule that passwords on all of their teens' social networks and apps be changed regularly and that passwords are not shared with anyone other than the parent. Fifth, parents should communicate to their children that, under no circumstances, do they post, tweet, or discuss where they are going, when they are away from home, and their current physical locations.[46] Finally, parents must monitor their teen's existence within the online community and must periodically check on their teen's activities while online.[47]

If a parent discovers that their child or teen is a victim of stalking or cyberstalking, parents must report the abuse to their local law enforcement community.[48] In addition, parents must mandate that their children cease to continue with their online and cell phone accounts and, if necessary, initiate new accounts within the online community.

STRATEGIES FROM LAW ENFORCEMENT

Since the majority of the ICAC reported to law enforcement involve either teens or preteens, the following is a list and discussion on strategies for parents with children navigating the online community. First, talk to your teens or preteens about school, their friends, their safety, and life in general. By having easy, light, and, casual conversations, the more significant conversations are less difficult. Second, talk to your children's friends when you visit them at school when they are riding in your vehicle, when they are in your home, and when you attending extracurricular events. Third, be present in the lives of your children. Know their teachers, know their friends' parents, attend their ballgames, attend parent night at school, and attend their band concerts. Fourth, explain to them about ICAC and laws related to ICAC. Fifth, require that you be a friend in the social networks, that you know their passwords, and monitor their online and cell phone activities.[49] Finally, trust but verify. If your child seems different lately, do not assume that it is simply teen years, ask them if there are things bothering them. If you do not ask, they may never tell.

Again, if you suspect your children are victims of an ICAC, ask them. Even a denial is not always a denial. If you suspect (or you know) that your children are victims of ICAC, report your suspicion either to your local law enforcement agency or online to the NCMEC.[50] Law enforcement will respond to your report.

In the meantime, based upon the type of ICAC you suspect, cancel or change online accounts for your child, cancel or change their cell number, and notify either cell phone providers or ISPs. As a customer of these services, you may request a log of activities; this is especially helpful for law enforcement in their investigations. In addition, provide to law enforcement the names and addresses (if available) of anyone you feel may be involved in these acts of victimization. Finally, talk to your child. Take them to meet with an investigator or a victim's advocate in order that you and your child know the process for addressing their ICAC.

SUMMARY

Child enticement, child solicitation, cyberbullying, cyberstalking, child trafficking, and child pornography are just some of the ICAC that exist today. Parents must be aware of these crimes against our children. As parents begin conversations with their children at an early age, and continue these conversations throughout the teen years, they are better able to protect their children. In turn, our children are better able to protect themselves from these forms of ICAC.

As a parent, we often ignore the impact we have upon the actions of our children. We often fail to remember that as the parent, we are legally responsible for our children until they reach the age of eighteen. In addition, we own their cell phones and usually pay for their access to the online community. With those responsibilities and ownership, we have the right to monitor their cell phone and online usage.

With sexting, probably the most common action, which is almost considered a norm in teen society, commanding that our teenagers not participate in sexting is probably a waste of time and language. However, in some few instances, based upon the relationships between teens and parents, conversations about the negative consequences of sexting may be enough to prevent the child from participating in sexting. Questions such as "Have you ever received a sext message?" or "Have you ever sent a sext message?" are both good questions to ask—however, as parent, you must be prepared to have your teen ask you the same questions. Other questions to ask "How well do you know the person you're sexting?" And "What would you do if your picture went public?" are also ways to initiate conversations about sexting if the questions are asked in a calm and causal manner. Of course, these will not be first-time conversations but rather conversations that are based upon over-the-years conversations on safety, teen life, and peer relationships.

For parents who have not had a pattern of "keeping you safe" conversations with their children, a first-time conversation on sexting as well as ICAC will most likely be difficult and awkward for both parties. In cases where parents and teens do not easily converse on the subject of sexuality, sexting and sexual exploitation may not be the best focus for the conversation. For these individuals, the concept of privacy and the right to privacy by their child may be a more appealing topic as related to ICAC. Regardless, parents should be aware of the conditions that exist within their teens' life prior to their involvement.

For teens today, it is more unusual for them not to have a cell phone and text than for them to have a cell phone and text. Parents must realize the experiences of today's teens and be willing to participate in computer and cell phone "spot checks" if they are concerned about the activities of their children. These attempts, just like with other discussions on proactive approaches to address ICAC, include open and continued lines of communication between the children and parents as well as parental supervision.

Tips from law enforcement are related to the communications between parents and their children. Tips include: talking to your teens or preteens about school, their friends, their safety, and life in general; talking to your children's friends; be present in the lives of your children, know their teachers and their friends' parents, attend their extracurricular events, explain to them about ICAC; require that you be a friend in the social networks and that you know their passwords in cyberspace; and trust your children but verify their stories. Lastly, if your children seem different lately, ask them if there are things bothering them.

Finally, parents must acknowledge that although they are proactive in protecting their children from ICAC, not all parents are proactive. Hence, parents should warn their children against distributing sexual language or sexual images to others. In addition, parents should warn their children against distributing text or images that generally report or document any form of illegal activity. Also, it should be noted that, for those teens without parental supervision, their vulnerabilities may increase the vulnerability in the teens with proactive parents. Since many ICAC are among peers, it will include not only your teen but also those teens at risk for victimization. Therefore, parents must communicate to their children their own willingness to help them if the child ever feels as though they are a victim of their own self-initiated sexting. By providing teens this safety net of acceptance and forgiveness, parents will be better able to protect their children from the dangers of ICAC.

Chapter Ten

Addressing Victimization

The victimization of their child is among the most horrifying of fears for a parent. As a parent, our job, above all, is to protect our children. Today, protection from harm includes not only the individuals we can see, but also, the individuals we cannot see, but who exist within cyberspace.

In January 2016, a thirteen-year-old girl in Virginia was found dead after sneaking out of her home to meet her eighteen-year-old "boyfriend," whom she had met online.[1] In 2015, a former Iraq veteran was convicted of extorting nude images (sextortion) from underage girls.[2] Also in 2015, three Michigan teens were convicted of sexting nude images of their peers (i.e., distributing child pornography).[3] Finally, in 2010, a Canadian teen posted a video in cyberspace that described her life as a victim of cyberbullying before she committed suicide.[4] Each of these cases involved the victimization of children in cyberspace and each of these cases involved someone's child.

As parents, our main concern is the safety and protection of our children. We teach our children to look both ways before they cross the street, to be cautious around fire and sharp objects, and about the dangers of strangers; however, in today's world of instant information and Internet searches, we often fail to teach our children about the dangers of cyberspace.[5] Cyberspace, the domain in which individuals utilize computers and other electronic devices to communicate via Internet or cell phone providers, is the new frontier for those seeking information and experiences. It is also the new frontier for individuals wishing to identify potential child victims for abuse and exploitation.[6]

This book was designed to be used as a parent's guide in the protection of their children in cyberspace what ICAC call extrafamilial or perpetrated by someone outside of the family. This book provides parents a description of the ICAC to include: child corruption, cases involving individuals who utilize the Internet and the online community to corrupt and recruit children for a variety of actions to include the perpetuation of hate; child pornography, the images or videos of children involved in sexual activity or sexually provocative dress; child sex rings, multiple children and multiple adult abusers; child sex tourism, tourism that involves the traveling of adults to locations outside of their home country for the intent to engage in any form of sexual contact with minors; child solicitation; child trafficking; cyberbullying, the use of cyberspace to intimidate, to embarrass, or to humiliate their victim; cyberstalking, the repeated use of technology to monitor, harass, intimidate, coerce, or frighten someone into an unwilling action; gross sexual imposition, forcing two individuals to have sexual contact with each other against their will; sexting and sextortion, the use of cyberspace to obtain through coercion sexual dialogues or pornography from another.

Historically, child abuse was not a subject for discussion. The sexual abuse of children was even less likely to be discussed and, if the perpetrator was a family member, the subject was taboo.[7] Later, the sexual abuse of a child is recognized as a crime of innocence and is of public concern. Today, child abuse within cyberspace is now gaining national attention.[8]

Every day there are thousands of confirmed victims of child abuse in the United States. Of those cases, many are victims within cyberspace. It is acknowledged that the information presented in this parent's book on child victimization within cyberspace is based upon information retrieved from cases of ICAC. However, many incidents of child abuse and exploitation via cyberspace remain unreported. Whereas there are no clear indicators of risk for child victimization in cyberspace, children from all ages and all backgrounds are potential victims.

LONG-TERM CONSEQUENCES

Researchers suggest that some of the long-term behavioral consequences of child sexual abuse demonstrated by adult survivors include low self-esteem, depression, anxiety, substance abuse, and somatization; these consequences also exist for ICAC involving sexual abuse and exploitation. However, these adults often feel the guilt and shame associated with survivors of adult sexual victimization, however, with deep-rooted feelings of worthlessness and self-blame as if they were merely inanimate objects with nothing of value to offer society.[9]

In addition, adult victims of child sexual abuse often find themselves unable to understand and participate in a "normal" adult sexual relationship. Conclusions differ as to whether intrafamiliar child sexual abuse is more traumatic than extrafamiliar child abuse; however, much research suggests that the source of the abuse is not as critical;[10] however, the more severe the abuse, the more damaging the effects for the survivor.

Adult victims of child sexual abuse often report a prevalence of nightmares and flashbacks as well as risks for adult victimization in terms of domestic violence.[11] Whether the adult assumes the role of the victim in the domestic setting or the abuser, the issues of power and control, evident in their childhood victimization, are again present in their adulthood.

Finally, for long-term behavioral consequences, delinquency and crime have been asserted to be related to traditional cases of child sexual abuse as well as ICAC. Running away from home and the area is not unusual for the young adult who is a victim. Prostitution, drug abuse, and sexual assaults are also not uncommon in the lives of adult survivors of child sexual abuse.[12]

In addition to long-term behavioral consequences, long-term physical consequences also often result from child sexual abuse. Long-term physical consequences of sexual abuse that have been identified in research include sexual dysfunction or a lack of interest in sex, physical health problems such as chronic pelvic infections and pregnancy complications, injuries related to the abuse, eating disorders, and addictions to alcohol, drugs, or prescription medicine.[13]

In summary, adults who have survived child sexual abuse have not only missed a healthy introduction to sexuality, they have also missed a healthy introduction to aging and adult relationships.[14] For many of these individuals the failure to control their victimization as a child leads to an obsessive control over their adult fate. For those who have lost the desire to maintain some sort of control over their lives (or feel as though they do not deserve control over their lives), the need to stay healthy and safe is absent.

THEORETICAL EXPLANATIONS FOR
CHILD EXPLOITATION IN CYBERSPACE

Researchers studying child abuse and ICAC have attempted to explain (not excuse) why anyone would use cyberspace to abuse a child. This book provided parents information on a variety of such crimes; however, explaining why individuals would continue to harm children remains a complex series of conditions, interacting dynamics, and events that may not ever be fully explained. By providing some sort of theoretical foundation, it is the goal of this chapter to not only assist parents in recognizing and providing assistance to the child who may be a victim of an ICAC, but also provide parents a foundation for understanding these crimes.

In early attempts to explain deviant behaviors, the notion of evil spirits or "the devils made me do it" was the cornerstone for such acts. This perspective, known as demonology, was first identified around 80 BCE and suggested that people committed evil deeds because of the influence of mysterious and evil supernatural powers. In effect, an abuser kills or exploits a child because they are possessed.[15] Although demonology as a perspective to explain evil actions was prevalent up until the eighteenth century, classical theory or choice perspective gave way to a process of considering and explaining evil behaviors that are the individual's choice.[16]

Under the Classical School of Criminology, political philosopher Cesare Beccaria (1738–1794), suggested that individuals acted of their own free will and that these actions were decided based upon careful considerations of which action would create more pleasure or more pain.[17] As applied to ICAC, if an individual decided to harm a child, then it was because the action would result in much pleasure for the abuser and little chance of pain.

Although the Classical School began over two centuries ago, it is still applied to criminal behaviors today in its contemporary form of Rational Choice Theory. For example, in the criminal action of child trafficking (discussed later in this text), a reasonable or rational offender would decide, based upon the potential for reward and punishment (pleasure and pain) whether or not they should traffic a child. If one considers that a child is a product, and the economic gain from the sale (such as trafficking) of that child is enormous, and that law enforcement has demonstrated limited efforts in arresting traffickers or even identifying victims of human trafficking, then rational choice perspective suggests that the abuser will make the decision to traffic a child.[18]

In discussions on problem-solving and choices, both inter-individual and intra-individual perspectives are applied to explain actions. From the inter-individual perspective, actions based upon interactions with others are explained; hence, certain demographic characteristics of the child (e.g., age) are attractive to their offender.[19] Intra-individual theories suggest that child abuse is the result of the offender's mental defect or a flaw in their genetic makeup.[20]

Sigmund Freud's (1856–1939) psychoanalytical approach suggested that mental disorders arose from conflicts within society and the instinctive needs of the individual. According to Freud, the individual's personality was based upon three distinct parts, or regions—the Id, the Ego, and the Super Ego.[21] The Id is one's natural drive with the demand for immediate gratification. The Ego is one's rational part and the Super Ego is the mediator and acts as the individual's conscience. This approach can be applied to pedophilia as a pedophile, by definition, is someone who is sexually attracted to prepubescent children; however, a child molester acts on those sexual desires. Some pedophiles who have the sexual attraction (Id) may never act on their desires as their ego and super ego are governing their desires.

Psychological explanations have been used often to rationalize or explain horrendous acts of criminal behavior. The criminal justice system use of the insanity defense is the solution. However, in most of these cases, the insanity defense is not successful.[22] Glandular and hormonal imbalances, adrenaline sensitivity, substance abuse, and even diet have also been associated with many different types of criminal behaviors. However, there exists much controversy with the application of biological theory, as it focuses on medical procedures to control sexual impulses of convicted offenders which many individuals label as inhumane.[23] For example, medroxyprogesterone is a synthetic hormone that lowers the blood serum testosterone levels in men and reduces their sexual interest, which is believed to reduce sex offender recidivism. Although there is some disagreement, there are some aspects of biochemical imbalance that have been widely accepted as the causation for criminal behavior and in particular crimes of a sexual nature against children. In addition, alcohol or other types of substance abuse are a significant factor contributing to abuse and exploitation.[24]

Just as there are individual-level (intra-individual) theoretical explanation for child abuse and neglect, there are also, inter-individual (macro-level or structural) explanations for the abuse, which include many of the earliest sociological theories as related to child abuse and exploitation. From this perspective, child abuse may be explained by examining the events that were external to the individual.

Differential association has been used to explain child abuse and exploitation as well as delinquency.[25] Abusive parents learn abusive behavior; thus, child abuse becomes an intergenerational phenomenon. Children who are abused or bullied at a young age are at a higher risk for repeating those behaviors. In addition, children who associate with older children may learn delinquent behavior and may also be subjected to abuse. In later research to explain child abuse from a sociological perspective, aggressive tendencies are learned rather than inborn in that children become hostile after witnessing aggressive behavior.

Control theories are based on the concept of why some people do not engage in criminal behaviors such as child abuse. From this perspective, theorists discuss two kinds of controls: personal and social. Personal controls involve individual conscience, commitment to law, and a positive self-concept, while social controls are concerned with social institutions such as family, schools, and religion. Containment theory stresses that inner and outer containment help prevent criminal behaviors.[26] Inner containment includes a positive self-concept, tolerance for frustration, and the ability to set realistic goals while outer containment includes institutions such as the family.[27] Negative self-concepts and low self-esteem have also been frequently noted as characteristics of those who abuse or exploit children. Finally, research suggests that individuals with low self-esteem are more likely to commit various types of offenses to include child abuse.

Specifically, those who have low self-control act impulsively and place their needs above the needs of the group—to include their need for pleasure. Thus, individuals who place their needs and desires above those of others are more likely to abuse a child if it is their desire.

Finally, Routine Activities Theory, developed by Cohen and Felson in 1979, argues that a person's activities or daily routines influence their likely victimization. This theory, based on three conditions, suggests that when conditions exist, victimization will occur. This victimization includes child abuse and neglect. The three conditions are: (1) a target, (2) motivated offenders, and (3) a lack of guardians.[28] A target is someone that another person might desire. In the case of individuals, the target may be someone easier to victimize, such as an elderly person or a child. Both individual types may be classified as vulnerable prey. What is it about these categories of victims that would make them vulnerable? Both may be considered physically weaker than their offender and may not have the ability to fend off an attack. Their lifestyle could also be a contributing factor to make them an attractive target, despite the elderly being considered the least likely segment of the population to be victimized. However, some children may be easier marks as their lifestyle may make them more accessible to a motivated offender.[29]

The motivated offender is anyone who is willing to victimize a potential target (i.e., a child) if they feel there is an attractive victim, and the opportunity to commit this crime exists due to a lack of guardianship. Under this condition, one must assume that given the correct conditions (internal or external) an individual exists who is willing to hurt another person or damage someone's property. In terms of child abuse, one assumes that there exist individuals motivated and willing to cause harm to a child for either personal pleasure or personal profit.

Finally, a lack of guardianship develops when individuals or conditions do not exist to intervene. For potential child victims, the presence of other individuals such as a police officer or a parent may be the guardian which prohibits their victimization. Unfortunately, when a child does not have anyone to serve as a guardian, victimization is possible.[30]

IDENTIFYING VICTIMS

Unfortunately for law enforcement, in most cases of ICAC, there are no physical indicators. This is, in part, because the abuse is not recognized or reported immediately. Since ICAC are rarely discovered through physical indicators, parents are usually in the best position to notice changes in their child's behaviors and actions.

In 1998, the NCMEC launched a Cyber Tip Line to further their mission of helping to prevent the exploitation of children in cyberspace.[31]

This tip line is especially significant in the reporting of ICAC as it provides an avenue of reporting ICAC for parents, the public, and electronic service providers. The NCMEC continually reviews cyber tip reports and refers those reports to law enforcement agencies. Parents will often utilize NCMEC for help if or when they discover or perceive their child to be a victim of an ICAC.

Generally, efforts to reduce the incidents of child abuse fall into one of the following three categories. The same may be applied to ICAC in the three categories of: (1) primary prevention, (2) secondary prevention, and (3) recurrence prevention.[32] Primary prevention efforts to prevent ICAC attempt to address the underlying causes such as the use of chatrooms and social media to facilitate adult-child interactions and conversations. Secondary prevention efforts target those individuals such as teens who are at risk for victimization through ICAC. Finally, tertiary efforts utilize an after-the-action model with victims of ICAC in an attempt to reduce the likelihood of repeated victimization. As this book has attempted to provide parents information to reduce child exploitation at both the primary and secondary levels, this chapter is an attempt to provide resources to parents of child victims of ICAC.

In 1998, the US Department of Justice and the OJJDP awarded ten law enforcement agencies the funds to design and implement a program (or task forces) to address the emerging issue of child pornography via the Internet. Currently, there are over 3,500 task forces comprised of local, state, and federal law enforcement agencies working together to identify, investigate, and prevent ICAC. For parents, recognizing potential cases of ICAC is critical in not only the investigation of the case but also in addressing the consequences of abuse for the child.

MY CHILD, THE VICTIM?

Most crimes against children in cyberspace are classified under the categories of either child sexual abuse or emotional abuse. However, emotional abuse, which results from crimes such as cyberbullying and sextortion, is also very likely to occur from an ICAC.

As parents, we presume that our children, if harmed, will reveal to us their victimization. Unfortunately, that presumption is often not correct in that children victims rarely provide clear accounts of their abuse and these children only subtly imply that something may have happened to them. For parents, the most critical question asked as related to ICAC, "Is my child a victim?," is often the most difficult to answer. For some children or teens, a positive response indicates the possibility of revealing their own initiated contact with their abuser. For other teens, a positive response indicates to others their vulnerability as a victim. Finally, for other teens, a positive response indicates an acknowledgment that someone that made them feel special is an abuser and the feeling of "I'm important to someone" will soon be over. Therefore, the teen may or may not acknowledge their abuse. Parents must be aware of potential physical and behavioral characteristics or indicators of ICAC abuse.

The first and most revealing indicators of ICAC abuse are physical indicators. Although physical indicators of sexual abuse are not common in most cases of child sexual abuse,[33] teen sexual abuse via ICAC may result in physical symptoms. The first sign of sexual abuse is not usually the initial evidence of sexual trauma, such as sperm or tears in the genital area, as assaults are rarely reported as soon as they occur. For teen victims, sexually transmitted diseases, urinary tract infection, or pregnancy are more common. Parents should be aware that immediate physical symptoms of these conditions are often the first indicators of sexual exploitation through ICAC.

A second physical indicator of exploitation through ICAC may be the presence of suspicious bruises.[34] Just as in cases of child physical abuse, bruises that are in unusual locations such as wrists or ankles as well as of unusual shapes such as those left by rope burns or cigarette lighters are also signs of potential ICAC. Parents should be aware of not only location of such bruises but also reasonableness of the explanation for the bruise and color of bruise as aging or healing of the trauma is reflected in its shading.

Finally, children with the propensity for self-harm may also be an indicator of victimization through ICAC.[35] For parents noticing the physical symptoms of body mutilation or cutting, loss of weight potentially through anorexia or bulimia, or branding through tattoos or piercing, a conversation on the potential for abuse is warranted. Just as with other types of child abuse, in some cases of exploitation, physical indicators are not apparent. Hence, parents should also be aware of behavioral indicators of potential victimization through ICAC.

Often a child or teen who is a victim of sexual exploitation from ICAC will display signs of that abuse through behavioral indicators. Just as teachers are trained on identifying signs of child abuse, parents should be aware of these indicators. A child or teen who is a victim of an ICAC may avoid others due to either embarrassment regarding their victimization or because their abuser has forced them to isolate themselves from others. In addition, teen victims of ICAC may appear angry, anxious, or depressed and may display a dramatic change in their overall personality and behaviors. The teens may also experience problems at school in terms of grades, attendance, or with authority figures such as teachers or other administrators. This problem with authority figures may also transfer to legal authorities such as law enforcement officers. It is also not unusual for child and teen victims of ICAC to use sexual language or descriptions of sexual acts in conversations with peers or to be involved in violent sexual or nonsexual relationships with peers. Finally, alcohol and drug use have also been associated with child and teen victims of ICAC.[36] The alcoholic or drug addicted teen, through their substance abuse, may escape their reality or memories for a while. However, for some victims of ICAC, once the effects of substance abuse are diminished, attempts at suicide or suicide are the last option. Parents must be aware of the potential victimization of their child to further protect their child.

HOW DO I REPORT MY CHILD'S ABUSE?

Anyone, including parents, may report potential cases of ICAC. Childhelp, the NCMEC, and departments of social services are three organizations that provide help for child victims. Other reporting organizations and their contact information are listed in Appendix A. Through many of these nationally recognized organizations, crisis assistance as well as counseling may be available for your child. In addition, parents may contact directly their local law enforcement agency.

Parents who report the exploitation to law enforcement officials may expect follow-up from the agency within the jurisdiction. Depending on the age of the child, law enforcement first-responders (e.g., patrol officers) will most likely record the initial report through a conversation with the parents and child. Law enforcement should not question your child without either your presence or your permission. After the initial report, an investigator or detective (depending upon the type of law enforcement agency) will follow up with more questions of the reporters (parents/child) as well potential questions to the accused (if identified).

Parents should be aware that the investigation of ICAC is different from traditional or one-on-one crimes against children and, as these crimes cross police jurisdictional lines, will often involve investigations from multiple law enforcement agencies; hence, ICAC are typically more time-consuming than traditional cases of child abuse. Once an offender is arrested, law enforcement's role in the case is diminished as the court or the prosecution process begins. Finally, for parents worried about the treatment of their child by law enforcement and the courts, the Victims' Rights Constitution Amendment of 1996 helps to ensure that all victims are treated with fairness, dignity, and respect.

HOW DO I HELP MY CHILD?

In the unfortunate event that your child has been a victim of ICAC, resources and efforts exist for assistance. After the initial report of abuse to law enforcement, the parents' focus will be on the healing of their child. The first part of healing, as suggested by most research in the area of victimization, is recognition of the crime and vulnerability.

For most parents, professional assistance from private counselors or school counselors as well as school officials is critical. Private counselors as well as school counselors are educated and trained in the developmental and social needs of children.[37] School officials are often able to reduce the likelihood of victimization within the school environment if they are made aware of the vulnerabilities. Therefore, these individuals provide much needed resources for parents who are unfamiliar with child psychology and victimization. In addition, often a child is more willing to work with an outsider than a family member in addressing their victimization.

In addition, just as it essential to control the physical environment in traditional forms of child abuse to prevent revictimization, it is essential to control the virtual community to prevent repeated victimization through

ICAC. Specifically, parents should limit or control their child's access to the online community. In addition, new accounts as well as user IDs and passwords should be established. Finally, new cell phone numbers should be obtained with instructions provided to the child or teen in terms of distribution of the new phone number.

SUMMARY

Today, cyberspace, which allows predators the opportunity to target children whom they have not met in person, plays a significant role in victimization. For parents, who are often at a loss when it comes to understanding the dynamics behind ICAC, the worry exists as to whether or not they are truly helping to keep their children safe. Through ICAC, child or teen victims may be enticed into many types of victimization to include sexual exploitation, cyberbullying, cyberstalking, and child trafficking.

Unfortunately, in most cases of ICAC, there is no physical evidence; thus, parents are usually in the best positions to notice changes in their child's behaviors and actions. In 1998, the NCMEC launched a Cyber Tip Line to further their mission of helping to prevent the exploitation of children in cyberspace. This tip line is especially significant in the reporting of ICAC. The NCMEC continually reviews cyber tip reports and refers those reports to law enforcement agencies. Hence, parents may utilize NCMEC or their local law enforcement agency if they discover or perceive their child to be a victim of an ICAC. A parent's job is to protect their children. For parents worried about the treatment of their child, the Victims' Rights Constitution Amendment of 1996 helps to ensure that all victims are treated with fairness, dignity, and respect.

Cases of children victimized in cyberspace involve a variety of offenders such as sexual addicts, child molesters, consumers of child pornography, child traffickers, and those involved in child sex rings. Through provided information and resources focused on ICAC as well as conversation with their children, parents are better able to provide assistance to their children to ensure their safety. This book was intended to be used as a guide for parents and the community who are interested in the protection of children. The children of today are worthy of our time, our resources, and our protection.

Information Sources for Reporting Internet Crimes Against Children

American Professional Society on the Abuse of Children
1706 E. Broad Street
Columbus, OH 43203
Phone: 614-827-1321
www.apsac.org

American Society for the Positive Care of Children (American SPCC)
6965 El Camino Real, #105-526
Carlsbad, CA 92009
http://americanspcc.org/

Association to Benefit Children
419 East 86th Street
New York, NY 10028
Phone: 212-845-3821
http://www.a-b-c.org/

Child Abuse Network (CAN)
2829 South Sheridan
Tulsa, OK 74129
http://www.childabusenetwork.org/

Child Abuse Prevention Foundation
2120 Diamond Boulevard, Suite 120
Concord, CA 94520
Phone: 925-798-0546
www.capc-coco.org

Children's Bureau
330 C St., SW
Washington, DC 20201
Phone: 202-205-8618
http://www.acf.hhs.gov/cb/

Childhelp: National Child Abuse Hotline
4350 E. Camelback Road, Building F250
Phoenix, AZ 85018
Phone: 480-922-8210
https://www.childhelp.org/hotline/

Child Welfare League of America
727 15th Street, NW, 12th Floor
Washington, DC 20005
Phone: 202-688-4200
http://www.cwla.org/

Darkness to Light
1064 Gardner Road, Suite 210
Charleston, SC 29407
Phone: 843-965-5444
http://www.d2l.org/site/c.4dICIJOkGcISE/b.6035035/k.8258/Prevent_
Child_Sexual_Abuse.htm#.WCC0UGorIdU

Kempe Children's Center
1825 Marion Street
Denver, CO 80218
Phone: 303-864-5254
www.kempecenter.org

Kids Matter Inc.
1850 N. Martin Luther King Drive, Suite 202
Milwaukee, WI 53212
Phone: 414-344-1220
http://www.kidsmatterinc.org/

National Alliance of Children's Trust and Prevention Funds
P.O. Box 15206 Seattle, WA 98115
http://www.ctfalliance.org/

National Association of Counsel for Children
13123 E. 16th Avenue, B.390
Aurora, CO 80045
Phone: 303-864-5320
www.naccchildlaw.org

National Center for Missing and Exploited Children
699 Prince Street
Alexandria, VA 22314
Phone: 800-the-lost
http://www.missingkids.org/home

National Clearinghouse on Child Abuse and Neglect Information
330 C Street SW
Washington, DC 20447
Phone: 800-394-3366
www.calib.com

National Committee to Prevent Child Abuse
2950 Tennyson Street
Denver, CO 80212
Phone: 877-224-8233
www.childabuse.org

National Criminal Justice Reference Service
Office of Justice Programs
810 Seventh Street SW
Washington, DC 20531
Phone: 202-307-5933
www.ncjrs.org

National Data Archive on Child Abuse and Neglect
College of Human Ecology
Cornell University

Ithaca, NY 14853
Phone: 607-255-7799
www.ndacan.cornell.edu

National Indian Child Welfare Association
5100 S.W. Macadam Avenue, Suite 300
Portland, OR 97239
Phone: 503-222-4044
http://www.nicwa.org/

Prevent Child Abuse America
228 South Wabash Avenue, 10th Floor
Chicago, IL 60604
Phone: 312-663-3520
www.preventchildabuse.org

The Natural Child Project
P.O. Box 3
Gabriola Island, BC V0R 1X0Canada
Phone: 866-593-1547
www.naturalchild.org

Notes

CHAPTER ONE

1. Abigail Hauslohner, "N.Y.C. Police Search for Man Who Tried to Set Four Women on Fire," *Washington Post*, September 14, 2016, accessed on November 20, 2016, https://www.washingtonpost.com/news/post-nation/wp/2016/09/14/n-y-police-search-for-man-who-tried-to-set-4-women-on-fire/?utm_term=.d29b8df6164e.

2. Sara Gregory, "2nd Virginia Tech Student Arrested in Nicole Lovell Case; Pond Searched," *Roanoke Time*, January 3, 2016, accessed on November 20, 2016, http://www.roanoke.com/news/crime/blacksburg/nd-virginia-tech-student-arrested-in-nicole-lovell-case-pond/article_f09f3259-4b3b-587e-87cb-3c07a3511230.html.

3. Department of Justice, *Former Navy Top Gun Instructor Found Guilty on Charges of Production of Child Pornography and Obstruction of Justice* (Washington, DC: U.S. Attorney's Office: Eastern District of Virginia, 2015).

4. David Byers, "'Do They See Nothing Wrong with This?': Bullying, Bystander Complicity, and the Role of Homophobic Bias in the Tyler Clementi Case," *Families in Society: The Journal of Contemporary Social Services* 94(4) (2013): 251–58.

5. Interpol, "Connecting Police for a Safer World," accessed November 23, 2016, https://www.interpol.int/Crime-areas/Crimes-against-children/Crimes-against-children.

6. Holy Bible, Genesis 22:10.

7. Holy Bible, Genesis 19:30–33.

8. Holy Bible, 2 Samuel 13.

9. Kimberly McCabe, *Child Abuse and the Criminal Justice System* (New York: Peter Lang, 2003), 5.

10. McCabe, *Child Abuse and the Criminal Justice System*, 6.

11. Kimberly McCabe and Daniel Murphy, *Child Abuse: Today's Issues* (Boca Raton, FL: Taylor and Francis, 2016), 146–60.

12. Cynthia Crosson-Tower, *Understanding Child Abuse and Neglect* (Boston: Allyn and Bacon, 2011), 145–68.

13. McCabe, *Child Abuse and the Criminal Justice System*, 42–43.

14. McCabe and Murphy, *Child Abuse*, 146–60.

15. John Walsh and Susan Schindehette, *Tears of Rage: From Grieving Father to Crusader for Justice: The Untold Story of the Adam Walsh Case* (New York: Simon and Schuster, 1998).

16. Amy Anderson and Lisa Sample, "Public Awareness and Action Resulting from Sex Offender Community Notification Laws," *Criminal Justice Policy Review* (2008): 371–96.

17. Joan Petersilia, "Parole and Prisoner Reentry in the United States," *Crime and Justice* (1999): 479–529.

18. Daniel Mears, Christina Mancini, Marc Gertz, and Jake Bratton, "Sex Crimes, Children, and Pornography Public Views and Public Policy," *Crime and Delinquency* 54(4) (2013): 532–59.

19. McCabe, *Child Abuse and the Criminal Justice System*, 47.

20. Indicators of School Crime and Safety, "Bullying at School and Cyberbullying Anywhere," 2014, US Department of Justice, School Crime Supplement to the National Crime Victimization Survey.

21. Robert D'Ovidio and James Doyle, "A Study on Cyberstalking," *FBI Enforcement Bulletin* 72(3) (2003): 10–18.

22. Amanda Lenhart, "Teens and Sexting," Pew Internet and American Life Project, December 15, 2009, accessed July 11, 2016, https://www.pewinternet.org/REports/2009/Teens-and-sexting.aspx.

23. Julie Herward, "To Catch All Predators: Toward a Uniform Interpretation of Sexual Activity in the Federal Child Enticement Statute," *American University Law Review* 63(3) (2014): 879–918.

24. McCabe and Murphy, *Child Abuse*, 146–60.

25. McCabe, *Child Abuse and the Criminal Justice System*, 40.

26. Kimberly McCabe, *The Trafficking of Persons: National and International Responses* (New York: Peter Lang, 2008), 4–7.

27. McCabe, *Child Abuse and the Criminal Justice System*, 40–44.

28. Walsh and Schindehette, *Tears of Rage*.

29. McCabe and Murphy, *Child Abuse*, 146–60.

30. Kimberly McCabe, "The Role of Internet Service Providers in Cases of Child Pornography and Child Prostitution," *Social Science Computer Review* 25(2) (2008): 1–5.

31. Mary Allen and Jillian Boyce, "Police Reported Hate Crimes in Canada," *Juristat: Canadian Centre for Justice Statistics* 1 (2013): 3–25.

32. Katie Mettler, "Why SPLC Says White Lives Matter Is a Hate Group but Black Lives Matter Is Not," *Washington Post*, August 31, 2016, accessed on October 23, 2016, https://www.washingtonpost.com/news/morning-mix/wp/2016/08/31/splc-the-much-cited.

33. Allen and Boyce, "Police Reported Hate Crimes in Canada," 3–25.

34. Allen and Boyce, "Police Reported Hate Crimes in Canada," 3–25.

35. Fox News, "Old Black Panthers vs. New Black Panthers Party," Fox News, July 8, 2010, accessed on October 23, 2016, http://nation.foxnews.com/black-panthers/2010/07/08/old-black-panthers-vs-new-black-panthers.

36. Kimberly McCabe and Olivia Johnston, "Perception on the Legality of Sexting: A Report," *Social Science Computer Review* 32(6) (2014): 765–68.

37. McCabe, "The Role of Internet Service Providers in Cases of Child Pornography and Child Prostitution," 1–5.

38. Kimberly McCabe, "Child Pornography and the Internet," *Social Science Computer Review* 18(1) (2000): 73–76.

39. Kimberly McCabe and Lacey Ore, "Pornography," in J. Greene's *Encyclopedia of Police Science*, 3rd ed., 1031–33 (New York: Taylor and Francis, 2007).

40. McCabe, *Child Abuse and the Criminal Justice System*, 81–84.

41. McCabe and Murphy, *Child Abuse*, 146–60.

42. McCabe and Murphy, *Child Abuse*, 146–60.

43. McCabe, *The Trafficking of Persons*, 75–86.

44. McCabe, *The Trafficking of Persons*, 4–7.

45. Pew Research Center, "What Do Parents Worry about Most?," March 28, 2016, accessed October 13, 2016, http://www.liljegreninjurylawyers.com/what-do-parents-worry-about-most/.

46. Indicators of School Crime and Safety, "Bullying at School and Cyberbullying Anywhere."

47. Kimberly McCabe and Gregory Martin, *School Violence, the Media, and Criminal Justice Responses* (New York: Peter Lang, 2005), 71–74.

48. D'Ovidio and Doyle, "A Study on Cyberstalking," 10–18.

49. Jenna Strawhun, Natasha Adams, and Matthew Huss, "The Assessment of Cyberstalking" *Violence and Victims* 28(4) (2013): 715–30.

50. SexOffenderAttorney.com, "What Is Gross Sexual Imposition? Penalties and Defense," accessed on July 11, 2016, http://www.sexoffenderattorney.com/resources/criminal-defense/sex-crimes/what-gross-exual-imposition-penalties-defense.

51. Lenhart, "Teens and Sexting."

52. Janis Wolak and David Finkelhor, *Sextortion: Findings from a Survey of 1631 Victims* (Druham: University of New Hampshire: Crimes against Children Research Center, 2016), 5–7.

CHAPTER TWO

1. Sara Gregory, "2nd Virginia Tech Student Arrested in Nicole Lovell Case; Pond Searched," *The Roanoke Time*, January 3, 2016, accessed on November 20, 2016, http://www.roanoke.com/news/crime/blacksburg/nd-virginia-tech -student-arrested-in-nicole-lovell-case-pond/article_f09f3259-4b3b-587e-87cb -3c07a3511230.html.

2. Department of Justice, "Former Navy Top Gun Instructor Found Guilty on Charges of Production of Child Pornography and Obstruction of Justice" (Washington, DC: U.S. Attorney's Office, Eastern District of Virginia, 2015).

3. Christina Hall, "Probation, No Cell Phones for 3 Teens in Sexting Case," *Detroit Free Press*, March 18, 2015, accessed on November 20, 2016, http://www .freep.com/story/news/local/michigan/macomb/2015/03/18/three-teens-sexting-case-macomb-county-sentenced-probation-chesterfield-township/24965503/.

4. Laura Liparbelli, "12-Year-Old Sentenced for Cyberstalking Classmate," *ABC News*, July 14, 2011, accessed on November 20, 2016, http://abcnews .go.com/Technology/12-year-sentenced-washington-cyberstalking-case/ story?id=14072315.

5. Darryn Beckstrom, "State Legislation Mandating School Cyberbullying Policies and the Potential Threat to Students' Free Speech Rights," *Vt. L. Rev.* (2008), 33, 283.

6. John Walsh and Susan Schindehette, *Tears of Rage: From Grieving Father to Crusader for Justice: The Untold Story of the Adam Walsh Case* (New York: Simon and Schuster, 1998).

7. Amy Anderson and Lisa Sample, "Public Awareness and Action Resulting from Sex Offender Community Notification Laws," *Criminal Justice Policy Review* (2008): 371–96.

8. Joan Petersilia, "Parole and Prisoner Reentry in the United States," 1999, *Crime and Justice*, 479–529.

9. Daniel Mears, Christina Mancini, Marc Gertz, and Jake Bratton, "Sex Crimes, Children, and Pornography Public Views and Public Policy," *Crime and Delinquency* 54(4) (2013): 532–59.

10. Janet Mullings, James Marquart, and Deborah Hartley, *The Victimization of Children: Emerging Issues* (Binghamton, NY: Haworth, 2003), 22–24.

11. David Strassberg, Ryan McKinnon, Michael Sustaita, and Jordan Rullo, "Sexting by High School Students: An Exploratory and Descriptive Study," June 2012, Archives of Sexual Behavior, accessed on January 17, 2016, http://www.researchgate.net/publication/225275306.

12. Kimberly McCabe and Daniel Murphy, *Child Abuse: Today's Issues* (Boca Raton, FL: Taylor and Francis, 2016), 146–60.

13. Maressa Brown, "Why Stranger Danger Doesn't Work: Tips for Keeping Kids Safe From Predators," July 10, 2014, accessed on November 7, 2016, http://thestir.cafemom.com/big_kid/174506/why_stranger_danger_doesnt_work.

14. Kimberly McCabe, "The Role of Internet Service Providers in Cases of Child Pornography and Child Prostitution," *Social Science Computer Review* 25(2) (2008): 1–5.

15. Federal Communications Commission, "Consumer Guide: Children's Internet Protection Act" (Washington, DC: Consumer and Government Affairs Bureau, 2013), 1.

16. David Finkelhor, "The International Epidemiology of Child Sexual Abuse," *Child Abuse and Neglect* 18(5) (1994): 409–17.

17. McCabe and Murphy, *Child Abuse*, 146–60.

18. Federal Communications Commission, "Consumer Guide: Children's Internet Protection Act," 1.

19. McCabe and Murphy, *Child Abuse*, 146–60.

20. Kimberly McCabe, *Child Abuse and the Criminal Justice System* (New York: Peter Lang, 2003), 32–38.

21. Kimberly McCabe and Gregory Martin, *School Violence, the Media, and Criminal Justice Responses* (New York: Peter Lang, 2005), 71–74.

22. McCabe and Murphy, *Child Abuse*, 146–60.

23. Cynthia Crosson-Tower, *Understanding Child Abuse and Neglect* (Boston: Allyn and Bacon, 2011), 145–68.

24. McCabe and Murphy, *Child Abuse*, 146–60.

25. Webopedia Guide, "Text Messaging and Chat Abbreviations, 2015," accessed on November 7, 2016, http://www.webopedia.com/quick_ref/textmessageabbreviations.asp.

26. McCabe, *Child Abuse and the Criminal Justice System*, 32–38.

27. Parents for Megan's Law, "Child Sexual Abuse: Who Are the Victims?" accessed on July 11, 2016, http://www.parentsformeganslaw.org/public/statistics_childSexualAbuse.html.

28. McCabe, *Child Abuse and the Criminal Justice System*, 32–38.

29. McCabe and Murphy, *Child Abuse*, 146–60.

CHAPTER THREE

1. W. Huang, M. Leopard, and A. Brockman, "Internet Child Sexual Exploitation: Offenders, Offenses and Victims," in *Crimes of the Internet*, F. Schmalleger and M. Pittaros, eds. (Upper Saddle River, NJ: Pearson, 2009), 43–65.

2. Kimberly McCabe, *Child Abuse and the Criminal Justice System* (New York: Peter Lang, 2003), 40–44.

3. Frank Schmallenger, *Criminology Today* (Upper Saddle River, NJ: Pearson, 2006), 472.

4. Maressa Brown, "Why Stranger Danger Doesn't Work: Tips for Keeping Kids Safe From Predators" July 10, 2014, accessed on November 7, 2016, http://thestir.cafemom.com/big_kid/174506/why_stranger_danger_doesnt_work.

5. Julie Herward, "To Catch All Predators: Toward a Uniform Interpretation of Sexual Activity in the Federal Child Enticement Statute," *American University Law Review* 63(3) (2014): 879–918.

6. SexOffenderAttorney.com, "What Is Gross Sexual Imposition? Penalties and Defense," accessed on July 11, 2016, http://www.sexoffenderattorney.com/resources/criminal-defense/sex-crimes/what-gross-sexual-imposition-penalties-defense.

7. SexOffenderAttorney.com, "What Is Gross Sexual Imposition?"

8. Huang et al., "Internet Child Sexual Exploitation."

9. David Finkelhor, *Child Sexual Abuse: New Theory and Research* (New York: Free Press, 1984).

10. Kimberly McCabe and Olivia Johnston, "Perception on the Legality of Sexting: A Report," *Social Science Computer Review* 32(6) (2014): 765–68.

11. McCabe, *Child Abuse and the Criminal Justice System*, 40–44.

12. Janis Wolak, David Finkelhor, and Kimberly Mitchell, "Internet-Initiated Sex Crime against Minors," *Journal of Adolescent Health* 35(5) (2004): 11–20.

13. McCabe and Johnston, "Perception on the Legality of Sexting," 765–68.

14. McCabe, *Child Abuse and the Criminal Justice System*, 32–38.

15. Kimberly McCabe, *The Trafficking of Persons: National and International Responses* (New York: Peter Lang, 2008), 4–7.

16. Amy Anderson and Lisa Sample, "Public Awareness and Action Resulting from Sex Offender Community Notification Laws," *Criminal Justice Policy Review* (2008): 371–96.

17. Darryn Beckstrom, "State Legislation Mandating School Cyberbullying Policies and the Potential Threat to Students' Free Speech Rights," *Vt. L. Rev.*, 33 (2008): 283.

18. Kimberly McCabe, "Child Pornography and the Internet," *Social Science Computer Review* 18(1) (2000): 73–76.

19. McCabe and Johnston, "Perception on the Legality of Sexting," 765–68.

20. Interpol, "Connecting Police for a Safer World," accessed November 23, 2016, https://www.interpol.int/Crime-areas/Crimes-against-children/Online -child-abuse-Q-As.

21. US Department of Justice, "Baton Rouge Man Convicted of Extorting Minors, Producing Child Pornography, and Receiving Child Pornography," January 7, 2016, accessed on October 27, 2016, http://www.justice.gov/usao-mdla/pr/ baton-rouge-man-convicted-possession-intent-distribute-heroin.

22. http://blogs.mprnews.org/newscut/2016/08/mn-court-of-appeals-weak ens-states-child-solicitation-law.

23. Ryan Dalton, "Abolishing Child Sex Trafficking on the Internet: Imposing Criminal Culpability on Digital Facilitators," *University of Memphis Law Review* 43(4) (2013): 1097–144.

24. Janet Mullings, James Marquart, and Deborah Hartley, *The Victimization of Children. Emerging Issues* (Binghamton, NY: Haworth, 2003), 22–24.

25. Finkelhor, *Child Sexual Abuse.*

26. David Finkelhor, "The Prevention of Childhood Sexual Abuse," *Future of Children* 19(2) (2009): 169–94.

27. Finkelhor, *Child Sexual Abuse.*

28. Finkelhor, *Child Sexual Abuse.*

29. Mullings et al., *The Victimization of Children*, 22–24.

30. Protect.org, "What Is the Magnitude of Child Exploitation?," accessed November 23, 2016, http://www.protect.org/articles/what-is-the-magnitude-of -child-exploitation.

31. Protect.org, "What Is the Magnitude of Child Exploitation?"

32. McCabe, *Child Abuse and the Criminal Justice System*, 81–84.

33. McCabe, *Child Abuse and the Criminal Justice System*, 40–44.

34. David Strassberg, Ryan McKinnon, Michael Sustaita, and Jordan Rullo, "Sexting by High School Students: An Exploratory and Descriptive Study," June 2012, Archives of Sexual Behavior, accessed on January 17, 2016, http://www .researchgate.net/publication/225275306.

35. McCabe and Johnston, "Perception on the Legality of Sexting," 765–68.

CHAPTER FOUR

1. Maressa Brown, "Why Stranger Danger Doesn't Work: Tips for Keeping Kids Safe From Predators," July 10, 2014, accessed on November 7, 2016, http://thestir.cafemom.com/big_kid/174506/why_stranger_danger_doesnt_ work.

2. Jessica Ringrose, Rosalind Gill, Sonia Livingston, and Laura Harvey, "A Qualitative Study of Children, Young People and Sexting: A Report Prepared for the NSPCC," July 2012, accessed on January 17, 2016, https://pdfs.semantic scholar.org/5c9a/3a395d869230b7972dca22e87642bb3dffcd.pdf.

3. Frank Schmallenger, *Criminology Today* (Upper Saddle River, NJ: Pearson, 2006), 481.

4. J. Augustine and J. Gomez-Duran, "Sexting: Research Criteria of a Globalized Social Phenomenon," *Archives of Sexual Behavior* 41(6) (2002): 1325–28.

5. Benjamin Wittes, Cody Poplin, Quinta Jurecic, and Clara Spera, "Sextortion: Cybersecurity, Teenagers, and Remote Sexual Assault," Center for Technology Innovation at Brookings, May 2016, 1–3.

6. Janis Wolak and David Finkelhor, *Sextortion: Findings from a Survey of 1631 Victims* (Durham: University of New Hampshire, Crimes Against Children Research Center, 2016), 5–7.

7. Augustine and Gomez-Duran, "Sexting," 1325–28.

8. Amanda Lenhart, "Teens and Sexting," Pew Internet and American Life Project, December 15, 2009, accessed July 11, 2016, www.pewinternet. org/2009/12/15/teens-and-sexting/.

9. Kimberly McCabe and Daniel Murphy, *Child Abuse: Today's Issues* (Boca Raton, FL: Taylor and Francis, 2016), 146–60.

10. David Strassberg, Ryan McKinnon, Michael Sustaita, and Jordan Rullo, "Sexting by High School Students: An Exploratory and Descriptive Study," June 2012, Archives of Sexual Behavior, accessed on January 17, 2016, http://www .researchgate.net/publication/225275306.

11. Kimberly McCabe and Daniel Murphy, *Child Abuse: Today's Issues* (Boca Raton, FL: Taylor and Francis, 2016), 146–60.

12. Lenhart, "Teens and Sexting."

13. Noel Diem, "Teen Sexting: What Are the Legal Consequences?," accessed November 23, 2016, http://lawstreetmedia.com/issues/law-and-politics/ teen-sexting-legal-consequences/.

14. US Department of Justice, "Citizens Guide to U.S. Federal Law on Child Pornography" (Washington, DC: Department of Justice, 2014), accessed on July 11, 2016, https://www.justice.gov/criminal-ceos/citizens-guide-us-federal-law -child-pornography.

15. Diem, "Teen Sexting."

16. Lenhart, "Teens and Sexting."

17. K. Martinez-Prathe and D. Vandiver, "Sexting among Teenagers in the United States: A Retrospective Analysis of Identifying Motivating Factors, Potential Targets, and the Role of a Capable Guardian," *International Journal of Cyber Criminology* 8(1) (2014): 21–35.

18. Kimberly Mitchell, David Finkelhor, L. Jones, and Janis Wolek, "Prevalence and Characteristics of Youth Sexting: A National Study," *Pediatrics* 129(1) (2012): 13–20.

19. Martinez-Prathe and Vandiver, "Sexting among Teenagers in the United States," 21–35.

20. Department of Justice, "Former Navy Top Gun Instructor Found Guilty on Charges of Production of Child Pornography and Obstruction of Justice" (Washington, DC: U.S. Attorney's Office: Eastern District of Virginia, 2015).

21. US Department of Justice, "Baton Rouge Man Convicted of Extorting Minors, Producing Child Pornography, and Receiving Child Pornography," January 7, 2016, accessed on October 27, 2016, http://search.proquest.com/criminaljusti ceperiodicals/printviewfile?accountid=12198.

22. Lenhart, "Teens and Sexting."

23. Jessica Ringrose, Rosalind Gill, Sonia Livingston, and Laura Harvey, "A Qualitative Study of Children, Young People and Sexting: A Report Prepared for the NSPCC," July 2012, accessed on January 17, 2016, www.pewinternet .org/2009/12/15/teens-and-sexting/.

24. Ryan Dalton, "Abolishing Child Sex Trafficking on the Internet: Imposing Criminal Culpability on Digital Facilitators," *University of Memphis Law Review* 43(4) (2013): 1097–144.

CHAPTER FIVE

1. Indicators of School Crime and Safety, "Bullying at School and Cyberbullying Anywhere," 2014, US Department of Justice, School Crime Supplement to the National Crime Victimization Survey.

2. O. Erdur-Baker, "Cyberbullying and Its Correlation to Original Bullying, Gender, and Frequent Risky Usage of Internet-Mediated Communication Tools," *New Media and Society* 10(11), (2010): 146–51.

3. Kimberly McCabe and Daniel Murphy, *Child Abuse: Today's Issues* (Boca Raton, FL: Taylor and Francis, 2016), 146–60.

4. Kimberly McCabe and Gregory Martin, *School Violence, the Media, and Criminal Justice Responses* (New York: Peter Lang, 2005), 23–25.

5. David Byers, "'Do They See Nothing Wrong with This?': Bullying, Bystander Complicity, and the Role of Homophobic Bias in the Tyler Clementi Case," *Families in Society: The Journal of Contemporary Social Services* 94(4) (2013): 251–58.

6. McCabe and Murphy, *Child Abuse*, 146–60.

7. McCabe and Martin, *School Violence, the Media, and Criminal Justice Responses*, 23–25.

8. Kimberly McCabe, *Child Abuse and the Criminal Justice System* (New York: Peter Lang, 2003), 81–84.

9. McCabe and Martin, *School Violence, the Media, and Criminal Justice Responses*, 71–74.

10. Pew Research Center, "What Do Parents Worry about Most?," March 28, 2016, accessed October 13, 2016, http://www.liljegreninjurylawyers.com/what-do-parents-worry-about-most/.

11. McCabe and Murphy, *Child Abuse*, 146–60.

12. A. Beale and K. Hall, "Cyberbullying: What School Administers (and Parents) Can Do," *The Clearing House* 18 (2007): 8–12.

13. Pew Research Center, "What Do Parents Worry about Most?"

14. Indicators of School Crime and Safety, "Bullying at School and Cyberbullying Anywhere."

15. McCabe and Murphy, *Child Abuse*, 146–60.

16. Janet Mullings, James Marquart, and Deborah Hartley, *The Victimization of Children. Emerging Issues* (Binghamton, NY: Haworth, 2003), 22–24.

17. "Parents for Megan's Law, Child Sexual Abuse—Who Are the Victims?" accessed on July 11, 2016, http://www.parentsformeganslaw.org/public/statistics_childSexualAbuse.html.

18. McCabe and Murphy, *Child Abuse*, 146–60.

19. Amy Anderson and Lisa Sample, "Public Awareness and Action Resulting from Sex Offender Community Notification Laws," *Criminal Justice Policy Review*, 2008, 371–96.

20. McCabe and Murphy, *Child Abuse*, 146–60.

21. Robert D'Ovidio and James Doyle, "A Study on Cyberstalking," *FBI Enforcement Bulletin* 72(3) (2003): 10–18.

22. McCabe and Martin, *School Violence, the Media, and Criminal Justice Responses*, 71–74.

23. McCabe, *Child Abuse and the Criminal Justice System*, 32–38.

24. McCabe and Murphy, *Child Abuse*, 146–60.

25. Erdur-Baker, "Cyberbullying and Its Correlation to Original Bullying," 146–51.

26. S. Hinduja and J. Patchin, "Social Influences on Cyberbullying Behaviors among Middle and High School Students," *Journal Youth Adolescence* 42(3) (2013): 711–22.

27. Erdur-Baker, "Cyberbullying and Its Correlation to Original Bullying," 146–51.

28. McCabe and Martin, *School Violence, the Media, and Criminal Justice Responses*, 71–74.

29. McCabe and Murphy, *Child Abuse*, 146–60.

30. B. Coloroso, *The Bully, the Bullied, and the Bystander* (New York: Harper-Collins, 2003).

31. Janet Mullings, James Marquart, and Deborah Hartley, *The Victimization of Children. Emerging Issues* (Binghamton, NY: Haworth, 2003), 22–24.

32. McCabe and Murphy, *Child Abuse*, 146–60.

33. A. Burgess, C. Regehr, and A. Roberts, *Victimology: Theories and Applications*, 2nd ed. (Burlington, MA: Jones and Bartlett Learning, 2013).

34. Beale and Hall, "Cyberbullying," 8–12.

35. Indicators of School Crime and Safety, "Bullying at School and Cyberbullying Anywhere."

36. Frank Schmallenger, *Criminology Today* (Upper Saddle River, NJ: Pearson, 2006), 481.

37. Kimberly McCabe and Olivia Johnston, "Perception on the Legality of Sexting: A Report," *Social Science Computer Review* 32(6) (2014): 765–68.

CHAPTER SIX

1. Jenna Strawhun, Natasha Adams, and Matthew Huss, "The Assessment of Cyberstalking," *Violence and Victims* 28(4) (2013): 715–30.

2. Daniel Mears, Christina Mancini, Marc Gertz, and Jake Bratton, "Sex Crimes, Children, and Pornography: Public Views and Public Policy," *Crime and Delinquency* 54(4) (2013): 532–59.

3. Robert D'Ovidio and James Doyle, "A Study on Cyberstalking," *FBI Enforcement Bulletin* 72(3) (2003): 10–18.

4. D'Ovidio and Doyle, "A Study on Cyberstalking," 10–18.

5. Pew Research Center, "What Do Parents Worry about Most?," March 28, 2016, accessed October 13, 2016, http://www.liljegreninjurylawyers.com/what-do-parents-worry-about-most/.

6. D'Ovidio and Doyle, "A Study on Cyberstalking," 10–18.

7. http://www.dailymail.co.uk/news/article-3761677/Teenage-girl-murdered-home-despite-warnings-police-stalked-obsessed-man.html

8. Benjamin Wittes, Cody Poplin, Quinta Jurecic, and Clara Spera, "Sextortion: Cybersecurity, Teenagers, and Remote Sexual Assault," Center for Technology Innovation at Brookings, May 2016, 1–3.

9. Janis Wolak, David Finkelhor, and Kimberly Mitchell, "Internet-Initiated Sex Crime against Minors," *Journal of Adolescent Health* 35(5) (2004): 11–20.

10. Wittes et al., "Sextortion," 1–3.

11. Stalking Resource Center, "Summary of Changes from VAWA 2013 Related to Stalking," (Washington, DC: Stalking Resource Center, 2014), 1–4. Accessed on October 11, 2016, http://www.victimsofcrime.org/docs/src/vawa -2013-and-stalking.pdf?sfvrsn=2.

12. D'Ovidio and Doyle, "A Study on Cyberstalking," 10–18.

13. Stalking Resource Center, "Summary of Changes from VAWA 2013 Related to Stalking."

14. Strawhun, Adams, and Huss, "The Assessment of Cyberstalking," 715–30.

15. Stalking Resource Center, "Summary of Changes from VAWA 2013 Related to Stalking."

16. Strawhun et al., "The Assessment of Cyberstalking," 715–30.

17. Stalking Resource Center, "Summary of Changes from VAWA 2013 Related to Stalking."

18. Wittes et al., "Sextortion," 1–3.

19. Janet Mullings, James Marquart, and Deborah Hartley, *The Victimization of Children: Emerging Issues* (Binghamton, NY: Haworth, 2003), 22–24.

20. Kimberly McCabe and Gregory Martin, *School Violence, the Media, and Criminal Justice Responses* (New York: Peter Lang, 2005), 71–74.

21. D'Ovidio and Doyle, "A Study on Cyberstalking," 10–18.

22. Protect.org, "What Is the Magnitude of Child Exploitation?," accessed November 23, 2016, http://www.protect.org/articles/what-is-the-magnitude-of -child-exploitation.

23. D'Ovidio and Doyle, "A Study on Cyberstalking," 10–18.

24. Strawhun et al., "The Assessment of Cyberstalking," 715–30.

25. http://www reuters .com/ article/us- crime- girl-cyber stalking-idUSTR E76 C74C20 110713.

26. David Finkelhor, Kimberly Mitchell, and Janis Wolak, *Online Victimization: A Report on the Nation's Youth* (Washington, DC: National Center for Missing and Exploited Children, 2000).

27. Kimberly McCabe and Daniel Murphy, *Child Abuse: Today's Issues* (Boca Raton, FL: Taylor and Francis, 2016), 146–60.

28. D'Ovidio and Doyle, "A Study on Cyberstalking," 10–18.

29. D'Ovidio and Doyle, "A Study on Cyberstalking," 10–18.

30. D'Ovidio and Doyle, "A Study on Cyberstalking," 10–18.

31. McCabe and Murphy, *Child Abuse*, 146–60.

32. Strawhun et al., "The Assessment of Cyberstalking," 715–30.

33. Pew Research Center, "What Do Parents Worry about Most?"

34. Finkelhor et al., *Online Victimization*.

35. Mullings et al., *The Victimization of Children*, 22–24.

36. McCabe and Murphy, *Child Abuse*, 150–55.

37. D'Ovidio and Doyle, "A Study on Cyberstalking," 10–18.

38. Mullings et al., *The Victimization of Children*, 22–24.

CHAPTER SEVEN

1. National Crime Prevention Council, "Tolerance for Teens" (MD: National Crime Prevention Council, 2016), accessed on October 23, 2016, http://www ncpc.org/topics/hate-crime/tolerance.

2. Kimberly McCabe, *Child Abuse and the Criminal Justice System* (New York: Peter Lang, 2003), 32–38.

3. Dustin Waters and Mark Berman, "Dylann Roof Found Guilty on All Counts in Charleston Church Massacre Trial," *Washington Post*, accessed on December 24, 2016, http://www.washingtonpost.com/news/post-nation/ wp/2016/12/15/jurors-begin-deliberating-in-charleston-church-shooting -trial/?utm_term=.050b543928cf.

4. Walter Bouman, "Best Practices of Hate/Bias Crime Investigations," *Law Enforcement Bulletin* 72(3) (2003): 21–25.

5. Mary Allen and Jillian Boyce, "Police Reported Hate Crimes in Canada," *Juristat: Canadian Centre for Justice Statistics* 1 (2013): 3–25.

6. Bouman, "Best Practices of Hate/Bias Crime Investigations," 21–25.

7. National Crime Prevention Council, "Tolerance for Teens."

8. Allen and Boyce, "Police Reported Hate Crimes in Canada," 3–25.

9. Bouman, "Best Practices of Hate/Bias Crime Investigations," 21–25.

10. Indicators of School Crime and Safety, "Bullying at School and Cyberbullying Anywhere," 2014, US Department of Justice, School Crime Supplement to the National Crime Victimization Survey.

11. A. Burgess, C. Regehr, and A. Roberts, *Victimology: Theories and Applications*, 2nd ed. (Burlington, MA: Jones and Bartlett Learning, 2013).

12. John Schafer and Joe Navarro, "The Seven Stage Hate Model," *Law Enforcement Bulletin* 72(3) (2003): 1–9.

13. Frank Schmallenger, *Criminology*, 3rd ed. (Boston: Pearson, 2016).

14. Schafer and Navarro, "The Seven Stage Hate Model," 1–9.

15. Katie Mettler, "Why SPLC Says White Lives Matter Is a Hate Group but Black Lives Matter Is Not," *Washington Post*, August 31, 2016, accessed on October 23, 2016, https://www.washingtonpost.com/news/morning-mix/ wp/2016/08/31/splc-the-much-cited.

16. http://www.nationalreview.com/article/437694/.

17. Emma Grown, "Two Teens Charged with Hate Crime for Video Threatening Black Classmate with Noose, Gun," *Washington Post*, April 11, 2016,

accessed on October 23, 2016, https://www.washingtonpost.com/news/education/wp/2016/04/11/two-teens-charged-with-hate-crime-for-video-threatening-black-classmate-with-noose-gun/?utm_term=.b29e213354bb.

18. Kimberly McCabe and Daniel Murphy, *Child Abuse: Today's Issues* (Boca Raton, FL: Taylor and Francis, 2016), 146–60.

19. FoxNews, "Old Black Panthers vs. New Black Panthers Party," Fox News, July 8, 2010, accessed on October 23, 2016, http://nation.foxnews.com/black-panthers/2010/07/08/old-black-panthers-vs-new-black-panthers-party.

20. Abigail Hauslohner, "N.Y.C. Police Search for Man Who Tried to Set Four Women on Fire," September 14, 2016, *Washington Post*, accessed on November 20, 2016, https://www.washingtonpost.com/news/post-nation/wp/2016/09/14/n-y-police-search-for-man-who-tried-to-set-4-women-on-fire/?utm_term=.d29b8df6164e.

21. McCabe and Murphy, *Child Abuse: Today's Issues*, 146–60.

22. Schafer and Navarro, "The Seven Stage Hate Model," 1–9.

CHAPTER EIGHT

1. Kimberly McCabe and Daniel Murphy, *Child Abuse: Today's Issues* (Boca Raton, FL: Taylor and Francis, 2016), 146–60.

2. Kimberly McCabe, *The Trafficking of Persons: National and International Responses* (New York: Peter Lang, 2008), 75–90.

3. Kimberly McCabe, *Child Abuse and the Criminal Justice System* (New York: Peter Lang, 2003), 32–38.

4. Allison Chawai, "The Disturbing Reality of Human Trafficking and Children," December 18, 2015, *Huffington Post*, accessed on October 19, 2016, http://www.huffingtonpost.com/allison-chawla-/disturbing-reality-human-trafficking_b_8831834.html.

5. McCabe, *Child Abuse and the Criminal Justice System*, 32–38.

6. McCabe and Murphy, *Child Abuse*, 146–60.

7. Ryan Dalton, "Abolishing Child Sex Trafficking on the Internet: Imposing Criminal Culpability on Digital Facilitators," *University of Memphis Law Review* 43(4) (2013): 1097–144.

8. Kimberly McCabe and Sabita Manian, *Sex Trafficking: A Global Perspective* (New York: Lexington Books, 2011), 147–58.

9. McCabe, *The Trafficking of Persons*, 75–90.

10. http://www.fox5dc.com/news/local-news/33056553-story.

11. McCabe, *Child Abuse and the Criminal Justice System*, 32–38.

12. M. Calder, *Child Sexual Abuse and the Internet: Tracking the New Frontier* (Frontier: Russell House, 2004).

13. Dalton, "Abolishing Child Sex Trafficking on the Internet," 1097–144.

14. McCabe and Manian, *Sex Trafficking*, 147–58.

15. McCabe, *The Trafficking of Persons*, 75–90.

16. McCabe and Manian, *Sex Trafficking*, 147–58.

17. Protect.org, "What Is the Magnitude of Child Exploitation?," accessed November 23, 2016, http://www.protect.org/articles/what-is-the-magnitude-of-child-exploitation.

18. McCabe, *Child Abuse and the Criminal Justice System*, 32–38.

19. McCabe and Manian, *Sex Trafficking*, 147–58.

20. McCabe, *Child Abuse and the Criminal Justice System*, 32–38.

21. McCabe, *The Trafficking of Persons*, 75–90.

22. Dalton, "Abolishing Child Sex Trafficking on the Internet," 1097–144.

23. W. Huang, M. Leopard, and A. Brockman, "Internet Child Sexual Exploitation: Offenders Offenses and Victims," in *Crimes of the Internet*, F. Schmalleger and M. Pittaros, eds. (Upper Saddle River, NJ: Pearson, 2009).

24. McCabe and Murphy, *Child Abuse*, 146–60.

25. McCabe, *Child Abuse and the Criminal Justice System*, 32–38.

26. McCabe, *The Trafficking of Persons*, 75–90.

27. Protect.org, "What Is the Magnitude of Child Exploitation?"

28. Chawai, "The Disturbing Reality of Human Trafficking and Children."

29. Calder, *Child Sexual Abuse and the Internet.*

30. Protect.org, "What Is the Magnitude of Child Exploitation?"

31. McCabe and Murphy, *Child Abuse*, 146–60.

32. McCabe and Manian, *Sex Trafficking*, 147–58.

33. Janis Wolak, David Finkelhor, and Kimberly Mitchell, "Internet-Initiated Sex Crime against Minors" *Journal of Adolescent Health* 35(5) (2004): 11–20.

34. A. Burgess, C. Regehr, and A. Roberts, *Victimology: Theories and Applications*, 2nd ed. (Burlington, MA: Jones and Bartlett Learning 2013).

35. McCabe, *The Trafficking of Persons*, 75–90.

36. Burgess et al., *Victimology.*

37. Frank Schmallenger, *Criminology Today* (Upper Saddle River, NJ: Pearson, 2006), 481.

38. "Babysitter Tattoos Children He Was Looking After . . . Then Parents Tried to Remove Inkings with a Hot Razor Blade When They Got Home," accessed December 4, 2016, http://www.dailymail.co.uk/news/article-2599711/Alexander-Edwards-tattooed-children.

CHAPTER NINE

1. Cynthia Crosson-Tower, *Understanding Child Abuse and Neglect*, 8th ed. (Boston: Allyn and Bacon, 2010).

2. Kimberly McCabe, *Child Abuse and the Criminal Justice System* (New York: Peter Lang, 2003), 32–38.

3. Janet Mullings, James Marquart, and Deborah Hartley, *The Victimization of Children: Emerging Issues* (Binghamton, NY: Haworth, 2003), 22–24.

4. Daniel Mears, Christina Mancini, Marc Gertz, and Jake Bratton, "Sex Crimes, Children, and Pornography: Public Views and Public Policy," *Crime and Delinquency* 54(4) (2013): 532–56.

5. Crosson-Tower, *Understanding Child Abuse and Neglect*, 145–68.

6. McCabe, *Child Abuse and the Criminal Justice System*, 32–38.

7. Kimberly McCabe and Daniel Murphy, *Child Abuse: Today's Issues* (Boca Raton, FL: Taylor and Francis, 2016).

8. McCabe, *Child Abuse and the Criminal Justice System*.

9. Mullings et al., *The Victimization of Children. Emerging Issues*, 22–24.

10. McCabe and Murphy, *Child Abuse: Today's Issues*.

11. Janis Wolak and David Finkelhor, *Sextortion: Findings from a Survey of 1631 Victims* (University of New Hampshire: Crimes against Children Research Center, 2016), 5–7.

12. Benjamin Wittes, Cody Poplin, Quinta Jurecic, and Clara Spera, "Sextortion: Cybersecurity, Teenagers, and Remote Sexual Assault." Center for Technology Innovation at Brookings, May 2016), 1–3.

13. Janis Wolak, David Finkelhor, and Kimberly Mitchell, "Internet-Initiated Sex Crime against Minors," *Journal of Adolescent Health* 35(5) (2004): 11–20.

14. Wittes et al., "Sextortion," 1–3.

15. Wolak and Finkelhor, *Sextortion*, 5–7.

16. O. Erdur-Baker, "Cyberbullying and Its Correlation to Original Bullying, Gender, and Frequent Risky Usage of Internet-Mediated Communication Tools," *New Media and Society* 10(11) (2010): 146–51.

17. A. Beale and K. Hall, "Cyberbullying: What School Administrators (and Parents) Can Do," *The Clearing House* 18 (2007): 8–12.

18. M. Calder, *Child Sexual Abuse and the Internet: Tracking the New Frontier* (Frontier: Russell House, 2004).

19. O. Erdur-Baker, "Cyberbullying and Its Correlation to Original Bullying," 146–51.

20. K. Martinez-Prathe and D. Vandiver, "Sexting among Teenagers in the United States: A Retrospective Analysis of Identifying Motivating Factors, Potential Targets, and the Role of a Capable Guardian," *International Journal of Cyber Criminology* 8(1) (2014): 21–35.

21. M. Medaris, and C. Girouard, *Protecting Children in Cyberspace: The ICAC Task Force Program* (Washington, DC: U.S. Department of Justice. Office of Justice Programs. Office of Juvenile Justice and Delinquency Prevention, 2002) (NCJ-191213).

22. Kimberly McCabe and Olivia Johnston, "Perception on the Legality of Sexting: A Report," *Social Science Computer Review* 32(6) (2014): 765–68.

23. McCabe and Murphy, *Child Abuse.*

24. John Schafer and Joe Navarro, "The Seven Stage Hate Model," *Law Enforcement Bulletin* 72(3) (2003): 1–9.

25. Kenneth Lanning, *Child Sex Rings: A Behavioral Analysis for Criminal Justice Professionals Handling Cases of Child Sexual Exploitation*, 3rd ed. (Quantico, VA: Federal Bureau of Investigation. Behavioral Science Unit, 1992).

26. David Finkelhor, *Child Sexual Abuse: New Theory and Research* (New York: Free Press, 1984).

27. Kimberly McCabe and Gregory Martin, *School Violence, the Media, and Criminal Justice Responses* (New York: Peter Lang, 2005), 71–74.

28. Finkelhor, *Child Sexual Abuse.*

29. G. Abel, "Self-Reported Sex Crimes of Non-Incarcerated Paraphilics," *Journal of Interpersonal Violence* 2(1) (1978): 3–25.

30. Children's Bureau, *Child Maltreatment 2013.* Washington, DC: U.S. Department of Health and Human Services, Administration for Children and Families, 2014.

31. Crosson-Tower, *Understanding Child Abuse and Neglect.*

32. Children's Bureau, *Child Maltreatment 2013.*

33. A. Pomponio, *Investigation and Prosecution of Child Abuse*, 3rd ed. (Thousand Oaks, CA: Sage, 2004).

34. McCabe, *Child Abuse and the Criminal Justice System*, 32–38.

35. McCabe and Murphy, *Child Abuse: Today's Issues.*

36. Mancini, C. *Sex Crime Offenders and Society* (Durham, NC: Carolina Academic Press, 2014).

37. McCabe and Murphy, *Child Abuse: Today's Issues.*

38. Abel, "Self-Reported Sex Crimes of Non-Incarcerated Paraphilics," 3–25.

39. Lanning, *Child Sex Rings.*

40. Wolak and Finkelhor, *Sextortion*, 5–7.

41. McCabe and Johnston, "Perceptions on the Legality of Sexting," 765–68.

42. Lanning, *Child Sex Rings.*

43. Mears et al., "Sex Crimes, Children, and Pornography: Public Views and Public Policy," 532–59.

44. Amanda Lenhart, "Teens and Sexting," Pew Internet and American Life Project, December 15, 2009, accessed July 11, 2016, https://www.pewinternet.org/REports/2009/Teens-and-sexting.aspx.

45. Robert D'Ovidio and James Doyle, "A Study on Cyberstalking," *FBI Enforcement Bulletin* 72(3) (2003): 10–18.

46. Mancini, *Sex Crime Offenders and Society*.

47. Lenhart, "Teens and Sexting."

48. D'Ovidio and Doyle, "A Study on Cyberstalking," 10–18.

49. S. Hinduja and J. Patchin, "Social Influences on Cyberbullying Behaviors among Middle and High School Students," *Journal Youth Adolescence* 42(3) (2013): 711–22.

50. Children's Bureau, *Child Maltreatment 2013*.

CHAPTER TEN

1. Sara Gregory, "2nd Virginia Tech Student Arrested in Nicole Lovell Case; Pond Searched," *The Roanoke Time*, January 3, 2016, accessed on November 20, 2016, http://www.roanoke.com/news/crime/blacksburg/nd-virginia-tech -student-arrested-in-nicole-lovell-case-pond/article_f09f3259-4b3b-587e-87cb -3c07a3511230.html.

2. Department of Justice, *Former Navy Top Gun Instructor Found Guilty on Charges of Production of Child Pornography and Obstruction of Justice* (US Attorney's Office: Eastern District of Virginia, 2015).

3. Christina Hall, "Probation, No Cell Phones for 3 Teens in Sexting Case," *Detroit Free Press*, March 18, 2015, accessed on November 20, 2016, http://www .freep.com/story/news/local/michigan/macomb/2015/03/18/three-teens-sexting -case-macomb-county-sentenced-probation-chesterfield-township/24965503/.

4. David Byers, "'Do They See Nothing Wrong with This?': Bullying, Bystander Complicity, and the Role of Homophobic Bias in the Tyler Clementi Case," *Families in Society: The Journal of Contemporary Social Services* 94(4) (2013): 251–58.

5. Kimberly McCabe and Daniel Murphy, *Child Abuse: Today's Issues* (Boca Raton, FL: Taylor and Francis, 2016).

6. Kimberly McCabe, *Child Abuse and the Criminal Justice System* (New York: Peter Lang, 2003).

7. J. Siegel, and M. Williams, "The Relationship between Child Sexual Abuse and Female Delinquency and Crime: A Prospective Study," *Journal of Research in Crime and Delinquency* 40 (2013): 71–95.

8. McCabe and Murphy, *Child Abuse*.

9. McCabe, *Child Abuse and the Criminal Justice System*.

10. Cynthia Crosson-Tower, *When Children Are Abused: An Educator's Guide to Intervention* (Boston: Allyn and Bacon, 2002), 35–38.

11. Cynthia Crosson-Tower, *Understanding Child Abuse and Neglect* (Boston: Allyn and Bacon, 2011), 145–68.

12. McCabe, *Child Abuse and the Criminal Justice System.*

13. Harvey Wallace, *Family Violence: Legal, Medical, and Social Perspectives* (Boston: Allyn and Bacon, 1999), 362–69.

14. J. Bund, "Did You Say Chemical Castration?" *University of Pittsburg Law Review* 59(1) (1997): 157–92.

15. Ronald Burke, *An Introduction to Criminological Theory* (Portland, OR: William Publishing, 2005).

16. M. Lanier and S. Henry, *Essential Criminology* (Boulder, CO: Westview, 1998).

17. Burke, *An Introduction to Criminological Theory.*

18. Kimberly McCabe, *The Trafficking of Persons: National and International Responses* (New York: Peter Lang, 2008), 4–7.

19. McCabe and Murphy, *Child Abuse.*

20. Bund, "Did You Say Chemical Castration?" 157–92.

21. Crosson-Tower, *Understanding Child Abuse and Neglect*, 145–68.

22. McCabe and Murphy, *Child Abuse.*

23. Janet Mullings, James Marquart, and Deborah Hartley, *The Victimization of Children: Emerging Issues* (Binghamton, NY: Haworth, 2003).

24. Wallace, *Family Violence*, 362–69.

25. A. Bandura, *Aggression: A Social Learning Analysis* (Englewood Cliffs, NJ: Prentice Hall, 1973).

26. Mullings, Marquart, and Hartley, *The Victimization of Children.*

27. David Gosselin, *Heavy Hands: An Introduction to the Crimes of Family Violence*, 4th ed. (Upper Saddle River, NJ: Prentice Hall, 2010).

28. McCabe and Murphy, *Child Abuse.*

29. McCabe, *Child Abuse and the Criminal Justice System.*

30. Crosson-Tower, *When Children Are Abused*, 35–38.

31. McCabe and Murphy, *Child Abuse.*

32. McCabe, *Child Abuse and the Criminal Justice System.*

33. I. Moyer, *Criminological Theories: Traditional and Nontraditional Voices and Themes* (Thousand Oaks, CA: Sage, 2001).

34. McCabe and Murphy, *Child Abuse.*

35. McCabe, *Child Abuse and the Criminal Justice System.*

36. M. Rocque, C. Posick, and T. Zimmerman, "Measuring Up: Assessing the Measurement Properties of Two Self-Control Scales," *Deviant Behavior* 34(3) (2013): 534–56.

37. Crosson-Tower, *When Children Are Abused*, 35–38.

Index

About the Author

Kimberly Ann McCabe, PhD, is director of the Center for Community Development and Social Justice and professor of Criminology at Lynchburg College. McCabe has been an expert witness in law enforcement policies and procedures, child abuse, school violence, human trafficking, and equity/parity/discrimination of employment in criminal justice and public safety agencies. She has also acted as a consultant for state and local agencies in the United States and the United Kingdom for design, implementation, and evaluation of criminal justice and public safety programs. She has authored many books and articles on child abuse, sex trafficking, and violence, including *Sex Trafficking: A Global Perspective* (2010) and *The Trafficking of Persons: National and International Responses* (2008).